PENGUIN PASSNOTES

Roots

Susan C⟨...⟩ ⟨Li⟩verpool and attended
Liverp⟨...⟩ ⟨...⟩oved
to Lon⟨...⟩ ⟨...⟩he has written a number of study guides
freelance ⟨...⟩ in Penguin Passnotes series, including *Pride and Prejudice*,
Silas Marner, *Kes* and *A Man For All Seasons*.

PENGUIN PASSNOTES

ARNOLD WESKER

Roots

SUSAN QUILLIAM
ADVISORY EDITOR: S. H. COOTE, M.A., PH.D.

PENGUIN BOOKS

Penguin Books Ltd, Harmondsworth, Middlesex, England
Viking Penguin Inc., 40 West 23rd Street, New York, New York 10010, U.S.A.
Penguin Books Australia Ltd, Ringwood, Victoria, Australia
Penguin Books Canada Ltd, 2801 John Street, Markham, Ontario, Canada L3R 1B4
Penguin Books (N.Z.) Ltd, 182–190 Wairau Road, Auckland 10, New Zealand

First published 1987

Interactive approach, developed by Susan Quilliam

The extract from 'Sometime it Happens' by Brian Patten
is printed by permission of Allen & Unwin.

'Marriage' by Gregory Corso is reprinted by permission of
Laurence Pollinger Ltd and New Directions Publishing Corporation.
Made and printed in Great Britain by
Richard Clay Ltd, Bungay, Suffolk
Filmset in 10/12 Monophoto Ehrhardt

Contents

To the Student

The purpose of this book is to help you appreciate Arnold Wesker's play, *Roots*. It will help you understand details of the plot. It will also help you to think about the characters, what the writer is trying to say and how he says it. These things are most important. After all, understanding and responding to plots, characters and ideas are what make books come alive for us.

You will find this Passnote most useful after you have read *Roots* through at least once. A first reading will reveal the plot and make you think about the life of the people it describes and your feelings for them. Now your job will be to make those first impressions clear. You will need to read the play again and ask yourself some questions. What does the writer really mean? What do I think about this incident or that one? How does the writer make such-and-such a character come alive?

This Passnote has been designed to help you do this. It offers you background information. It also asks many questions. You may like to write answers to some of these. Others you can answer in your head. The questions are meant to make you think, feel and respond. As you answer them, you will gain a clearer idea of the play and of your own ideas about it. When your thoughts are indeed clear, then you will be able to write confidently because you have made yourself an alert and responsive reader.

The page references are to the edition of the play published by Penguin Books. *Roots* is in the book called *The Wesker Trilogy*, which also contains *Chicken Soup with Barley* and *I'm Talking About Jerusalem*.

Background to the Play

Before reading *Roots*, you may well wonder what sort of person wrote it. After studying the play, the question is probably even more in your mind. Was it a Norfolk playwright, concerned with showing Norfolk life on the stage? A country person, intent on exploring the world he knows and loves?

The answer is neither of these, although *Roots* itself is based on Arnold Wesker's own experience. In fact, he is the Ronnie of the play (Beatie Bryant is Wesker's own wife, Dusty), and many of the things we learn about Ronnie throughout *Roots*, and in the other plays in the same series, where he actually appears on stage, are true of Wesker.

Like Ronnie, Arnold Wesker was born of Jewish parents in the East End of London. His mother, Leah Perlmutter, and father, Joseph Wesker, were refugees who came to England to escape persecution in their own country. They settled among the Jewish community of Stepney and it was there that young Arnold grew up, among an atmosphere of militant Jewish Communism.

He attended a series of Jewish schools in the East End, and also joined the Young Communist League and the Zionist Youth Movement. It was inevitable that, in those days, many of the persecuted Jews should turn to political parties which stood for what the ordinary people wanted. The idea of power in the hands of the working classes was an attractive one to people who had suffered so much and so helplessly because they had no power over their own fate. In earlier plays of Arnold Wesker's, *Chicken Soup with Barley* for example, he goes into great detail about the Jewish Communist movement. In *Roots*, Ronnie's Socialist ideas, which we hear about through Beatie, reflect the same sort of thinking, only perhaps in not quite so extreme a way.

When Arnold Wesker left school at the age of sixteen, he took a series of different jobs, each one extending his ability to think for himself. Many were jobs which involved a craft or manual skill of some sort – he worked as a furniture-maker's apprentice, a carpenter's mate – but he also worked in several bookshops. In 1950 he did his National Service, a spell in the armed forces which was compulsory for all young men for a period after the Second World War. Arnold joined the Air Force, and it was here that he had his first taste of acting.

After National Service, he once more worked in a bookshop, and then moved to Norfolk to stay with his sister, and take a number of jobs – seed sorter, farm labourer, kitchen porter. When he came back to London he worked as a pastry-cook, and then went to Paris, again to work in a restaurant.

He used his experience as a cook to write one of his plays, called *The Kitchen*, and you may remember that in Act 1 of *Roots*, Beatie speaks of meeting Ronnie when he worked as a cook in the kitchen of a Norfolk hotel.

Throughout every job he took, however, Arnold's passion for words survived. If you have an impression from *Roots* that Ronnie is a person who talks and talks, revels in speaking and writing, loves words and how to use them, you are most certainly seeing Arnold Wesker too. His love of the spoken and written language found its real expression in 1958 when, with the support of an Arts Council grant, his work began to be recognized. *Chicken Soup with Barley* was the first play of his to be performed, and was the first of the trilogy which also includes *Roots* and *I'm Talking About Jerusalem*. All three were great successes, and Arnold Wesker's career as a leading playwright began.

Since those early days in the late 1950s, there seem to have been three main strands to Wesker's life. His personal life revolves around his family; as mentioned earlier, the love affair that prompted the writing of *Roots* resulted in Wesker's marriage to the Beatie of the play, Dusty Bicker. Their relationship together, with their four children, has been a focal point of his life.

The early ideals, that began in Stepney with the Young Communist League, have also influenced him. In 1961, his commitment to the Nuclear Disarmament Campaign led to his being imprisoned for a short while. Socialist principles have shone through in many of his plays, and sometimes resulted in their not being accepted in society.

The strand of his life for which Wesker is most famous is, however, his ability to write. Since 1959 he has written a steady stream of plays for the English stage, sometimes for film and TV, and has also directed his own work in a wide variety of foreign countries, and even in foreign languages. Other theatrical projects have occupied him, too; in the early 1960s, together with a number of other young British playwrights, he founded Centre 42, a theatre project aimed at bringing plays to the ordinary people. He has also written a large number of articles, critiques and some short stories.

And what of Ronnie? In *Roots*, we leave him, as Beatie does, at the end of the play, a figure never met in the flesh, but very alive in our minds. He stops as the play stops, in his mid-twenties, a Socialist, an intelligent, working-class writer, who gives up his girlfriend because, 'It wouldn't really work would it?' At that time, the parallels with Arnold Wesker were real; Ronnie was a self-portrait, and Arnold Wesker was an intelligent, working-class writer.

But time passed. Ronnie stayed frozen in the play, but Arnold Wesker grew older and developed. The Socialism has become mellowed with age, the writing has brought him fame and fortune. He has married Beatie Bryant. And perhaps what is all too easily forgotten is that, unlike Ronnie, Arnold Wesker is a living person, working steadily to produce plays that reflect not the ideals and ideas he had when he wrote *Roots* or *Chicken Soup with Barley* but the stage of personal and professional development he has reached now, thirty years later.

An Interview with Arnold Wesker

The door is opened by a tall, good-looking blonde woman, who urges me inside with a smile and a 'Come in quickly – it's cold!' I step into a dark lobby and am directed upstairs; 'Go straight on up until you reach the top.'

The 'top', four floors up, turns out to be an attic room. No one is there, so I look around at walls covered with posters, pictures, photographs, books. The desk is laden with books, an electric typewriter hums quietly. Sheet after sheet of manuscript cover the chairs, the sofa, the floor. I bend forward to read the latest dramatic masterpiece, only to find myself reading a recipe. Wesker writing cookery books?

'It's my wife's book, not mine,' a voice behind me explains proudly, and Arnold Wesker arrives, small, well-built, dark, close-shaven and bursting with energy. He speaks quickly and enthusiastically, emphasizing and savouring each word, but throwing it out, as if he hasn't quite enough time for all he wants to say. When it comes to talking about *Roots*, both the enthusiasm and the energy double.

'How did I come to write *Roots*? Well, the whole thing actually happened.' Used to authors who spend years inventing plots, not taking them ready-made from real life, I look startled. 'My wife, Dusty, *is* Beatie Bryant. She's a Norfolk girl.' So the story is not invented to illustrate a series of ideas or ideals? No, on the contrary, Wesker explains, *Roots* was taken from a real-life experience. He and Dusty courted, lived in London for a while – and yes, he did nearly break the relationship off. 'I thought it wouldn't work.' But it did work, and in comes Dusty, the door-opening lady of downstairs, armed with coffee and biscuits, living proof that Wesker, unlike Ronnie, did not act the 'coward'. The play, he says smilingly, was his wedding present to Beatie Bryant.

Was *Roots* then simply an account of real events, with no thought of making a point? No, neither really – 'My skill is in recognizing the points life makes which are worth – to my mind – handing on.' For Wesker, writers fall, roughly, into two categories: those who begin with ideas and then invent characters and plots to illustrate these ideas, and those who begin with experience and use their writing to organize that and offer it for the use and delight of the onlooker. The play, for him, is about Beatie's growth, her development through her experiences, her 'rebirth and re-realization'. He comes back, again and again, to the mid-point of the play, describing vividly how he imagines the scene where Beatie emerges from the bath. For him, that is the moment when she really sees herself for the first time, extraordinary and beautiful, almost like Venus, newborn from the waves.

But the final scene too is important, as the point where Beatie at first seems to fail, to lose everything – and then breaks through to a new strength, a new 'magnificence', as Wesker calls it. *Roots* is the only one of his plays, he tells me, where this happens, where he allows a character to rise again after failure. I wonder whether this accounts for its popularity. Maybe, says Wesker.

Beatie is the centre of the play, but what of the other characters? Wesker repeats the comment he makes at the start of the text of *Roots*, that he is not disgusted with the people in his plays, just 'annoyed' with them – perhaps because they are real people? Yet, and he emphasizes this, all of them too have their moment of glory, the one point in the play when they act in a totally magnificent way. Afterwards, they may fall back into mediocrity and failure, but for that one moment they are magnificent. For Mrs Bryant, it is championing, easily and without a thought, the friend arrested for accosting men. For Jimmy, it is cheerfully cleaning up the old alcoholic. Even the minor characters have their moment of glory; Frankie for example, in his spontaneous and surprisingly sympathetic outburst in defence of the girl in the moral tale, 'Blust woman, she were in love!'

What other ideas are important in the play? Certainly the whole issue of the working class, and how it settles for mediocrity, is vital. Wesker himself was born working class, a fact he seems proud of. He speaks almost nostalgically of his younger days, his fight for Socialism, his championing of the working classes. But somehow, that and his love of individuality didn't go well together. He is full of belief in society, but the reality of working-class rule has so often clashed with his desire for the freedom of the individual. 'Maybe that's why my belief in Socialism faded . . .'

Why is *Roots* a play? Why not a novel or a poem? I have already guessed, from the sheer delight he takes in the way people struggle to make language from their thoughts, that to write a piece for the spoken word is what Wesker enjoys most. Hence, not a novel.

In fact, *Roots* is poetry and play combined. Wesker points to the posters round the wall, one of a performance in Denmark next to one of a first night in Paris beside a group of photos of Dusty. The same sort of 'shock', putting one image next to another, can be found in poetry, explains Wesker. This is the effect he has tried to achieve in *Roots*. So conversations between characters are often short, the subject changes often, and the very difference causes an almost physical jolt, that affects the audience as poetry can – and as Wesker wants it to. We move gently from the play back to the man. What do we need to know about him, in order to understand his work? 'That I have an anarchistic temperament . . . that I'm Jewish.' By anarchy, he doesn't mean he enjoys chaos. On the contrary, he believes in order. 'After all – that's what art is, the ordering of chaos.' But he prefers to see people impose their order rather than have society impose it. His anarchism led him in his youth to go to jail for the cause of nuclear disarmament.

The same desire to fight for freedom, to be a 'free spirit' is seen in his Jewishness. He knows, though he never experienced, the wartime cruelties, the ghettos. He will fight for freedom, for people, for individuality throughout his life, as Ronnie does in his way, and as Beatie does in hers.

We've talked for two hours now, thrown ideas round the room, filled the time with words. I get the impression that ideas and words, spoken and written, are what he lives for. And it is the living word, not past words, that excite him. Though he may have written *Roots*, though he may now be trying, in this interview, to help others understand and respond to it, he is genuinely concerned that it is made clear that *Roots* was thirty years ago, a past time of his life.

For Wesker himself has moved on. He has made a career as a playwright, a moulder of words. He has had numerous plays, articles and prose pieces produced in England and all over the world. His work has been published, produced, translated, reproduced, re-published.

So, as I make my way back down the flights of stairs again and out into the cold, I realize that although I came to see the author of *Roots*, I have in fact met someone very different. For *Roots* was then. Arnold Wesker is now.

Summary of the Plot

The play is set in Norfolk in the 1950s and centres round one family, the Bryants, particularly one daughter, Beatie.

ACT 1

Act 1 is set in the home of another Bryant daughter, Jenny, and her husband, Jimmy. The house is untidy and run down, but Jenny seems cheerful, as she comforts her baby daughter and does the washing up (p. 85). Jimmy comes in. He is suffering from back pain, which Jenny says is indigestion.

The married couple's chat is interrupted by the arrival of Beatie, Jenny's sister (p. 86). She is staying in Norfolk on holiday, and her boyfriend Ronnie will join her in a fortnight, to meet the Bryant family. Beatie makes herself at home, talking easily to Jimmy and Jenny, reading some comics left lying about (p. 87).

Beatie talks a lot about her boyfriend Ronnie, particularly about what he says and thinks of her actions. She seems to feel that his opinion is more important than anything else – his opinion of her reading, her fight for benefits, the way she argues with him (pp. 88–90).

Jenny and Jimmy are embarrassed at Beatie's outspokenness, and the talk turns to simple gossip about neighbours and Jimmy's allotment (p. 92). As the girls wash up, the conversation is about working conditions in London and in the country. Here again Beatie causes friction, by challenging Jimmy's planned march in a Territorial Army parade when, she claims, he knows nothing about the politics of the country he's supposed to be defending (pp. 93–4). Jimmy becomes annoyed, and goes off to his allotment.

Left alone, the girls talk about Beatie's relationship once again. Beatie tells her sister how she met Ronnie, slept with him and followed him to London. Now, though, she is unable to live his sort of life, learn what he has to teach her, even though she loves him (p. 95).

But, says Beatie, she won't need to know things when she's married to Ronnie and busy looking after their children. The conversation then turns to Jenny's little daughter, who is illegitimate. Jimmy married her in spite of this, and Jenny still has told nobody who the child's father is (p. 96).

Beatie suddenly notices how untidy the house is, and starts cleaning it up. Jenny joins in, and the two girls rampage around the house, tidying and also talking about the quarrels between various members of the family – which leads them on to remember their own squabbles when they were children (pp. 97–9). Beatie asks how her father and mother are, and Jenny says that Mr Bryant gives his wife very little money for the housekeeping (p. 100).

The girls' conversation is interrupted by sounds outside. Jenny's neighbour, Stan Mann, is being brought home drunk by Jimmy (p. 101). When Jimmy eventually comes in, he explains how he met Stan at the allotment, sluiced him down after he messed himself and kindly brought him back. At this point Stan himself comes in, says hallo to Jenny, and embarrasses Beatie by asking why she's not married yet (pp. 102–103).

Jimmy takes Stan home again, and when he comes back, the family get ready for bed. Jimmy goes straight off, armed with a newspaper, but the girls stay at the door talking to one another for a while. Eventually they go to bed, and the curtain falls on a darkened room and moonlight (pp. 103–104).

ACT 2, *Scene 1*

The scene is set in Beatie's parents' house, two days later. Mrs Bryant is at the door of the neat cottage, calling the cat. Giving up, she goes back to peeling potatoes, when Stan Mann walks in (p. 106).

Mrs Bryant greets him kindly, and they chat. Stan defends his own drinking, and rants on about the younger generation not enjoying life to the full. He himself is sickening for a cold, and Mrs Bryant sends him off home to take care of himself (pp. 107–108).

Left alone, Mrs Bryant listens to the radio. Soon, Beatie arrives (p. 108) and says hallo to her mother; the two women chat on about Beatie's luggage and the bus she came on (p. 109).

Beatie tells her mother that Ronnie is coming to see the family – she is worried he won't approve of the Bryants, and nags her mother about the family quarrels, the way her mother speaks, the bowl she does the washing-up in (p. 110). Beatie once again starts quoting Ronnie, standing on a chair and proclaiming like a preacher, until the wasps in the room distract her. She and her mother go on a wasp hunt (p. 111).

Then, while her mother heats the water for Beatie to have a bath, the two chat on. Beatie shows her mother some of the paintings she has done (p. 112), after which both women begin to prepare food. When Beatie starts singing a song Ronnie has taught her (p. 113), Mrs Bryant mentions a popular love song, which Beatie thinks is sickly. But she sings it to her mother, trying to get the older woman to react to the words and what they mean, sharing her worries about a similar lack of communication between Ronnie and herself (pp. 114–15).

The sound of an ambulance disturbs them, and then a moment later, Mr Bryant comes in. He and Beatie greet each other, and Mr Bryant, home early because of stomach ache (p. 116), says that he found Stan Mann collapsed by the side of the road; the ambulance was taking him to hospital (p. 117).

Mr Bryant's boss, Mr Healey, comes to enquire why Bryant has left work early (p. 118). He seems polite but business-like, and expects Bryant to be back at work by the afternoon. He also mentions that Stan Mann has died, which saddens all the family (p. 119).

Beatie and her father begin to argue, he saying that it is a waste of electricity for her to cook a cake for her sister (p. 120). Mrs Bryant joins with Beatie in arguing, but the old man is firm, and the two women give in, though Beatie is near tears and Mrs Bryant speaks bitterly of her marriage. Finally, Beatie goes to get a present she has bought for her father, and throws it in his lap (pp. 121–2). The family sit down to lunch.

ACT 2, *Scene 2*

After lunch, Mr and Mrs Bryant are still not speaking to each other, and communicate through Beatie (p. 122). She gets tired of this, and asks her father to fetch the tin bath, and her mother to put up the curtains to give her privacy. Beatie is going to get dressed up and go across to see her brother Frank and his wife.

Once Mr Bryant has gone off back to work (p. 123), the two women prepare the bath, and Beatie gets undressed. Mrs Bryant tells her daughter about Jimmy Skelton, a village man who has been arrested, while Beatie talks about Ronnie and his work (p. 124). Once again, Beatie complains when comparing Ronnie's style of life with that of her family, and although she listens to her mother's gossip, it is obvious that her mind is really on Ronnie (p. 125).

As Mrs Bryant chatters on, Beatie gets out of the bath (p. 126) and stands looking at herself in the mirror as she tunes the radio to some classical music. Beatie almost seems to see herself for the first time at this, the mid-point of the play. She gets very angry when her mother turns the music off, and accuses Mrs Bryant of hindering her development by never caring whether her daughter learned things, or opened her mind to what was happening outside (p. 127).

In the end, in desperation, Beatie makes her mother sit and listen as she puts some classical music on the new record-player she has bought (p. 128). As she listens, Beatie herself becomes excited by the music and dances; as the curtain falls, catching her daughter's enthusiasm, Mrs Bryant too smiles and claps her hands (p. 129).

ACT 3

It is two weeks later, and the whole family is due to arrive for tea on the day Ronnie comes to stay. We can now see the front room of the cottage, with a table spread with food.

Beatie is upstairs changing, and calls down to her mother nervously, asking about the food (p. 130) and the time, telling her mother to hurry. Mrs Bryant eventually goes upstairs to change.

After a moment, the Bryants' son Frank and his wife Pearl come in. Beatie calls from upstairs and Frank immediately starts asking her about Ronnie (p. 131). When Beatie comes down, the three young people talk about family quarrels again, particularly why Pearl and Mrs Bryant are not on speaking terms (p. 132).

Jimmy and Jenny come in, and Frank starts asking Jimmy whether he has started an association he was talking of in the pub recently – to allow people who are not having enough sex to meet each other. Frank finds the idea funny (p. 133), but Jimmy is embarrassed.

The talk turns back to Ronnie; the family are all curious to know what he is like, sure that he is a strange person, unlike them (p. 134). Then Mr Bryant comes in from work, and Mrs Bryant emerges, now wearing her best frock.

At first no one notices that Mr Bryant is upset, but he then tells them that he has lost his job, been put on casual labour. The family sympathizes, but only Beatie is really upset (p. 136).

The talk turns to Stan's death, and how 'Mrs Mann' is coping with it. The couple were not married, but 'Mrs Mann' gave up her job to look after Stan (p. 136).

Frank reads from the paper a piece about a London boy assaulting an old lady. When Mrs Bryant gets angry about the violence, Beatie challenges her ability to know what justice is all about.

Mrs Bryant doesn't know what to say (p. 137), and this gives Beatie a chance to criticize her once again; they very nearly quarrel.

Mr Bryant comes in, smartly dressed, and this breaks up the argument – the family immediately begin to gossip again as if nothing has happened (p. 138), but Beatie is not so easily put off.

She tells the family a story, a 'moral problem' (p. 139), challenging them to say who was most to blame. When she has finished the story, of a girl who is seduced and abandoned, the family don't know how to react to her (p. 140). They blame first one person in the story, then another, until Beatie caps everything by telling them what Ronnie thinks. She works herself up into a frenzy of argument (pp. 141–2), until eventually she's stopped by a knock at the door.

Beatie happily goes to answer it, thinking it is Ronnie arriving. It turns out to be a parcel for her mother – and a letter from Ronnie breaking off their relationship. Mrs Bryant grabs the letter from Beatie and reads it out, to everyone's embarrassment (p. 142).

Beatie is stunned. She starts to remember, and regret, all the times she didn't listen to Ronnie, didn't accept the opportunities he was giving her. Mrs Bryant too accuses her, of not being all the things she should have been in the relationship (p. 143), of being unable to hold a relationship together.

Turning on her family, now, Beatie says that they didn't support her (p. 144), but Mrs Bryant retorts that Beatie spent so much time telling her family what they were doing wrong that she didn't notice what they were doing right. Also, she accused them of all the things she did herself, the things that, in fact, finally ended the relationship (p. 145).

Shattered, Beatie turns on herself, saying that she and the rest of the Bryants have no roots, no means of supporting themselves with knowledge, pride, growing. She remembers hearing her sister Susan say she wouldn't mind dying if the bomb dropped – and comments on what that shows about the way everyone is living life, bored and useless (p. 146). So much so that artists and musicians, people who create the beauty of art and communication, expect people to be uninvolved and unintelligent, and don't bother creating true beauty for ordinary people (p. 147).By this time, the family has lost interest. They turn away to sit at the table and eat. But Beatie has realized something that changes her whole attitude – that she is for the first time thinking for herself, developing her own ideas and speaking about them. Now that the relationship has ended, she is doing what Ronnie always wanted her to do – speaking for herself. She realizes this with sudden amazement and joy, as the curtain falls and the play ends.

Commentary

The pages before the actual play begins give us some information which, when we understand it, introduces us to the play.

We find a list of the characters, each with a note saying who he or she is. All but two of the characters are members of the same family, the Bryants. In fact, we learn from the play itself that there are other members of the family whom we hear about but who never appear.

Write out a family tree for the Bryant family. Include on it all the characters we meet in the play, and the ones we hear about. If you write the family tree out on a large sheet of paper, you can add to it any details you learn about the characters as you read the play.

Arnold Wesker adds a note about his characters, that they should not be played as caricatures – over-exaggerated. What do you think he means by this? What could be the dangers of playing the characters in an over-exaggerated way?

Arnold Wesker also notes that he is not disgusted with the people he writes about, but he is annoyed with them. Once you are sure you understand the play, you might like to ask yourself what reasons Wesker has to be annoyed, and whether you yourself find that the characters he writes about are annoying.

We also find directions as to the setting of the play, time and place. *Roots* is set in 'the present', the time the play was actually written, the late fifties. Can you remember any other references in the play to fashions, music, dances, that would tell you that the play was set at that time?

The action of the play stretches over two weeks. It begins on the day that Beatie Bryant comes back to her family for a short holiday, which will have as its high spot the arrival of her boyfriend Ronnie. Two weeks later, on the day her Ronnie is due to arrive, he ends the relationship, and the play finishes with Beatie's response to this.

The setting of the play is Norfolk. On a map, find out where Norfolk is. It is a rural county, most of the work there being farming and hand-crafts. The country people, at least at the time the play was written, were not well off, and had an independent, rather defensive attitude towards outsiders.

Also, they used a particular Norfolk dialect, and Arnold Wesker adds a note on this too, helping the reader understand what the words mean. For further help, turn to the glossary on page 89 in this book. Because it is easier to understand the people in the play if you understand the language they speak, it is a particularly good idea when studying *Roots* to go to a live performance of the play. This will help you hear the words of the play as they would be spoken in a true Norfolk accent.

ACT 1: *Scene Setting*

Arnold Wesker takes quite a few lines to describe the setting of the first act, a house in Norfolk belonging to Jenny and Jimmy Beales. When you read the description, you should start to form a clear picture of the stage setting. You might even want to draw a plan or picture of the way you imagine the stage would be laid out. If you do this, make sure that you read the whole of this act, and include in your plan or drawing all the scenery and props needed during the act.

By reading this description, you may also begin to learn something about Jenny and Jimmy even before you meet them, what sort of people they are, whether they are rich and poor, even what sort of class they are (pp. 85–6).

Jenny herself is on stage, washing up. We have a description of her and her character that adds to what we already know. And when she begins to speak, answering her little girl who is crying for a sweet, we learn even more. Write down five words that you think describe Jenny and the sort of person she is. Try not to use words that Arnold Wesker has already used to describe her.

Now Jenny's husband Jimmy comes in. He too is described; make another list of five words about Jimmy.

The chat between husband and wife is like a lot of the conversation

in the play. It drifts from one topic to another, and often back again
to the first, providing an interesting contrast as one subject is set next
to another. The talk is seldom very emotional, and often repeats what
has been said before. Despite this, Jimmy and Jenny talk comfortably,
as if they are easy with each other.

Jimmy complains about his back, and Jenny supports him by offering him his tea, and saying she told her mother about the pain. But
she doesn't fuss over him, and Jimmy doesn't seem to expect her to.
He is quite sharp about her mother's suggestion that it is indigestion.

Jimmy mentions seeing Doctor Gallagher, and Jenny is amazed,
for she knows the doctor has cancer, and would not have thought he
would have lived so long.

Read over the conversation and stage-directions in this small section
between Jenny and Jimmy and begin to form an impression of the
sort of relationship they have. Would you say it is intense, or casual;
full of friction or easy-going? Within the relationship, what is Jenny's
position? Is she free and independent, or oppressed? What role does
she take in the family? Finally, review what you know about each of
their characters, and begin to form a picture in your mind of both
Jenny and Jimmy. (pp. 85–6)

A voice off-stage signals the arrival of Beatie, Jenny's sister, come
to stay for a few days. Beatie is the heroine, the most important
figure in the play, so try to get a good idea, from the first time we see
her, of what sort of person she is. She's described as 'ample, blonde,
healthy-faced' (p. 87). Read the conversation between her and the
other two characters on pages 87–8, and then see if you can pick out
of the following list the words that apply to Beatie.

pleased to see Jenny	intelligent
forthright	patient
friendly	relaxed
shy	likes her food
at ease with Jimmy's teasing	independent
aggressive	

What does the way Beatie comes in and makes herself at home tell
you about the family links between the three characters? Do you
think Jenny and Beatie are the same sort of person – are there any
family likenesses? How does Jimmy react to Beatie?

We also find out almost immediately that Beatie is engaged but not yet married; how does she react when Jimmy questions her about this, and what does this show you about her and her relationship? (pp. 88–91)

Beatie picks up a comic and starts to read it, commenting that this is something she always does when she gets home. She begins, from Jenny's questions, to think about how this compares with the time she spends in London, and in particular with the life she lives with her boyfriend, Ronnie.

You'll notice that throughout the play Beatie quotes Ronnie, reminds us of what he has said to her, acts as if she is him. The stage direction tells us that 'we see a picture of him through her' (p. 88). This is important. We not only get to see Ronnie, but we see him 'filtered' through Beatie's impressions of him. The fact that she loves and admires him comes through clearly, and also that she resents him. You might like to wonder why Arnold Wesker chose to present Ronnie to us like this, rather than have him appearing as one of the characters on the stage.

Read through Beatie's accounts of Ronnie over the pages 88–91. What do you learn about him? Make a list under the following headings.

his attitude to Beatie
his attitude to comics
his attitude to quarrelling
his attitude to words

You'll notice that we learn hardly anything about his physical appearance – why do you think this is? On the other hand, we learn a lot about his opinions and attitudes. Do you think you'd like him if you met him?

In particular, look again at the section where Beatie talks about 'bridges'. What does she (or Ronnie) mean by 'bridges'? Why are they so essential?

You learn a great deal too about Beatie in this section. Can you answer these questions?

What does Beatie think about Ronnie?
Does she admire him?
Does she love him?

Does she enjoy her sex-life with him?
Do you think she wants to marry him?
What does Beatie think about herself?
Does she admire herself?
Whom does she admire most – herself or Ronnie?

You should by now be getting some impression of the sort of relationship they have together. Is it a relationship you would want to be part of? Why? Why not? (pp. 90–2)

Jimmy and Jenny have not been quite sure about what Beatie has been saying about Ronnie. Their responses have changed from confusion to sarcasm to anger. When Beatie ends her description of Ronnie's behaviour when they argue with a comment about their making love, there is an embarrassed silence. Beatie, knowing she is teasing them both, carries on talking about love in the afternoon, and Jimmy wonders whether she takes time off from work for it.

What do you learn about the attitude to sex of all three characters from this small incident? Beatie is certainly at ease with the thought of making love, the other two – though married – are embarrassed. They drop the subject quickly.

The next moment, they are all enjoying the homemade ice-cream, joking about pink milk. Then the talk turns to a neighbour who has been gored by a bull. Finally, Beatie asks Jimmy about his allotment and how it's going. Notice how often Arnold Wesker moves his characters from one topic to another, showing us more about each by the contrast.

What does the movement from sexuality to ice-cream to injury to allotments show us about the family, and each character in it? What do you learn about their attitudes to life? Are they really without sexuality? Do they really not care about Dickie Smart's accident?

Also, what does talking about such things do for the three characters, and their family life?

Next time you are sitting with a group of people, maybe your family, who are chatting, listen carefully to what they are saying. Are they talking about anything in particular, or anything important? Does their topic of conversation change as often as it does for the characters in the play?

Do they talk as unemotionally, or do the people you listen to get very heated about some things? Which kind of conversation do you prefer – the kind in the play, or the one you were part of? Which do you think is more useful? (pp. 91–4)

The women start to wash up; do you think it's fair that Jimmy shouldn't help them? What is he doing at the same time?

As they work, there is silence, broken by spasmodic conversation. Arnold Wesker comments, in his stage directions, that such silences need 'organizing'. Why do you think he says this – what might happen if the silences on stage were allowed to just drift on in an unorganized way?

Arnold Wesker also adds a comment about the way his characters live. Read the passage, which probably contains the most direct comment on character in the play. What is Wesker saying here? For each of these questions, choose the answer that seems most appropriate.

1. Wesker says that the people in the play
   a. might as well be dead.
   b. do not live with much intense emotion, except for Beatie.
   c. live intensely, except for Beatie.
   d. live intensely but show no sign of it.

2. The characters live
   a. a routine life because they do the same jobs day after day.
   b. in a routine that never ceases to amaze them.
   c. a life that follows the routine of nature.
   d. following the routine of nature and accepting things that happen.

3. The people in the play do all the following EXCEPT
   a. talk in fits and starts.
   b. talk quickly.
   c. talk as if there were an audience there.
   d. talk about important things.

4. The characters
   a. have no affection for each other.
   b. show no affection but are attached to each other.
   c. only feel affection when one of them dies.
   d. only feel upset when there is a death.

When the conversation starts again it is about political things; there has been a strike in London. Read the section from the middle of page 92 to the middle of page 93, where they talk about the strike. Decide what each character thinks about working conditions and the right to strike. Then complete these sentences:

Beatie feels strikes are . . .
She wishes farm workers would . . .
She thinks Mr Bryant . . .

Jimmy feels the bus workers' strike was . . .
He thinks the farm workers are . . .
He is afraid that . . .

Notice how Jimmy is inconsistent in his attitude, feeling one way about the strike and another about his own working conditions. He then tells Beatie about being in a Territorial Army parade in London during the coming year. Beatie is not impressed. While she hands out the presents she has bought for the family, she says that Jimmy's efforts won't do any good if an atom bomb is dropped.

How do you think Jimmy feels about Beatie's comment? How does he reply? He and Beatie start an argument, Jimmy defending what he is doing, Beatie trying to explain to him that he knows very little about the country he is supposed to be fighting for.

Notice how the argument develops, Jimmy defending, Beatie asking him questions which only get him more annoyed as he cannot answer them. Finally he goes for her, directly telling her not to make him feel uncomfortable by talking about ideas he doesn't understand.

What does this scene show us about both Beatie and Jimmy? Read it through and make a list of five more things you learn about each character, to add to your previous list of five. In particular, look at the way Beatie answers back, not trying to shame Jimmy, but equally not being intimidated by him.

In fact, if you have read the play before, you will notice that Beatie carries on doing just what Jimmy warns her not to, and that because of this, she loses the family's sympathy when she most needs it. On the other hand, notice how when Jimmy returns, he ignores what has happened between them, and treats Beatie just as kindly as before. (pp. 92–4)

When Jimmy leaves, Beatie is upset at having hurt him. She immediately sees the similarity between the way she and Jimmy have quarrelled and the way she and Ronnie interact.

Beatie is very aware of the way she is, and particularly of how she doesn't take advantage of what Ronnie is offering her. She admits to being stubborn, not wanting to learn from him, and she says she gets her stubbornness from her mother. Ronnie is only too willing to give her what she needs to learn and to join in with the conversations that he and his friends have, but she will not give in. Do you think she ought to?

But when Jenny comments that it doesn't seem as if Beatie and Ronnie have much of a relationship, Beatie denies this. She tells of how they first met, courted, and developed their relationship. How did these things happen? Put these sentences in order to form an account of what happened.

a. Ronnie went back to London.
b. Beatie was working as a waitress in the Dell Hotel.
c. Ronnie felt he was responsible for Beatie.
d. Ronnie was working in the kitchen of the Dell Hotel.
e. Beatie fell in love.
f. Beatie and Ronnie slept together.
g. Beatie followed him to London.
h. Beatie chased Ronnie with compliments and presents.
i. Beatie let Ronnie think he couldn't leave her.
j. Beatie and Ronnie stayed together in London.

When you read the speech where Beatie remembers how she and Ronnie started going out together, how do you imagine she feels when she says these words? Can you picture her, on the stage, the look on her face, the tone of her voice? What does this tell you about the way she felt about Ronnie then?

Why do you think she slept with him? What do you feel about her statement that she let him think he was responsible for her because she wanted him to stay with her? Do you think better or worse of Beatie for doing this?

How does Beatie feel about Ronnie now? Has she really any regrets? Does she feel there are any parts of the relationship that are not what she would like? Jenny warns Beatie that the differences between her and her fiancé are very great, and they probably won't be happy together. Beatie argues with her. Who is proved right in the end?

When you read this section, you can probably get some idea not only of Beatie's character, and how she feels about Ronnie, but also of Ronnie's personality and how he feels about Beatie. What sort of person do you think he is – would you like him if you met him? What do you think he feels about Beatie? Why do you think he slept with her?

What differences are there between Ronnie and Beatie? Complete these sentences and then write a paragraph about the difference between them.

. . . seems more independent than . . .
. . . likes talking more than . . . does.
. . . writes a great deal; . . . doesn't.
. . . thinks about politics and art, whereas . . . never thinks about them.
. . . isn't interested in learning, whereas . . . is interested in . . .

Despite all these differences, Beatie says in the end that she loves Ronnie. What do you think she means by this – how does she know she loves him? Do you think he loves her? Is there any hint at this stage that they might break up in the end? If you met Beatie at this stage in the play, what advice would you give her about her relationship? (pp. 94–6)

With a sudden change of mood, Beatie offers to show Jenny how to bake pastries – Ronnie has shown her, in spite of the fact that she resented it.

As Jenny lights the Tilley lamp to brighten up the room, Beatie comments that she and Ronnie will be all right once they are married, for then she'll be looking after the children, and won't need to worry about learning things. Do you think she is right?

Mentioning children leads Jenny to comment on her own, and Beatie to ask if she is going to have any more. We learn that Daphne is Jenny's child by someone else, and that Jimmy married her despite that. This may make you see the couple in a totally different light; how does it change your view of them to know:

that Jenny slept with someone before marriage?
that Jenny has an illegitimate child?
that she won't tell anyone who the father is?
that Jimmy married her knowing this?
that they plan to have children of their own?

What do you think Jenny means when she says that she doesn't believe in love; she seems to be saying that she and Jimmy got married without loving each other. How is her view of love different from that of Beatie, talked about on page 96? (pp. 96–7)

From two contrasting conversations about sex, marriage and love, we turn to the realities of building a home – or rather, having problems in building it. Beatie suddenly realizes what a mess the house is in, tells Jenny off, and then starts to tidy up. The two girls begin to clear away, all the time talking about the Bryant family.

Once again, there are a series of snippets about various people. Who are they talking about when they say these words?

'. . . won't know where (the bike) is . . .'
'. . . she and Mother don't talk to each other . . .'
'. . . she's so bloody fussy she's gotten to polishing the brass overflow pipe . . .'
'. . . someone . . . who always wanted more'n she got . . .'
'. . . you got everything . . .'
'. . . (she) sent it to Susan through the fishmonger what live next door her in the council houses . . .'
'. . . wasn't good enough for (him)'

Who is the only member of the family who isn't mentioned in this conversation? Why do you think this is?

What do you learn about the family, the way they have got on in the past, and the way they get on with each other now? What do you learn about each of their characters?

Do you think that, overall, they were a happy family in the past – and now? Does the way they behave, talk about each other, feel about each other remind you of your family, or the family of anyone you know? Have you ever had a conversation like the one in this scene with one of your family, complaining about other relatives? What did you say and feel?

As this section of the scene finishes, the room is clear, and Beatie grabs a broom to sweep up. It is almost as if, having talked about her family, she has cleared away bad feelings just as she has tidied up the room. There only remains one other member of the family to gossip about, and that is her father, Mr Bryant. (pp. 97–100)

When Beatie asks, Jenny tells her that their father is still very tight with money. Is it their mother Jenny is concerned about, as Mr

Bryant gives her hardly anything to keep house with? Beatie guesses how much, and is over-generous in her guess. Notice though how Jenny mentions all the 'luxuries' Mrs Bryant indulges in, including some gambling on the Pools and the Tote.

Why do you think Arnold Wesker includes this part of the conversation; what do we learn from it? These are some reasons why he might have included it – choose the ones you think are correct, and complete the sentences with proof of what you are saying.

Arnold Wesker includes this section

to show us more about Mr Bryant's character . . .
to show us Beatie's attitude to her father . . .
to show us Jenny's attitude to her mother and father . . .
to show us something about Mrs Bryant's character . . .
to say something about the position of women in those days . . .

The little scene finishes with the news that Pearl, the girls' sister-in-law, won money on the Tote. Such wins seem to be important in the Bryant family life. Why do you think this is?

What impression, throughout the last few pages, have you begun to form about the life the Bryants lead? Would you say they were rich or poor; would you say they were of the working class or the managerial class? (pp. 100–101)

As the girls finish talking, they hear Jimmy returning with a drunk old man. Jenny says it is a neighbour of theirs, Stan Mann, who has been paralysed, but nevertheless gets very drunk all the time. She speaks of how Stan Mann has come down in the world because of his drinking, and how he has lost all he had.

When Jimmy comes in, he backs up Jenny's story of the old man drinking a fortune away. He also tells the girls how Stan came up to him at the allotment, and as he bent down to pick up a carrot, messed his trousers. Jimmy immediately cleaned the old man up with a hose, wrapped an old sack round him and brought him home. What does this show you about Jimmy?

You should have a pretty clear picture of him by now, and this incident with Stan Mann will tell you something else you need to know. Write a paragraph about Jimmy as you see him at this point in the play; what sort of person is he? Would you get on with him if you met him? (pp. 101–102)

Now Stan Mann himself arrives, a little sobered up, and hobbling, with a stick. He apologizes to Jimmy, who tells him to go off to bed, then says hallo to Jenny. At first he doesn't recognize Beatie standing next to her sister, but then he tells her off for putting on weight, neatly insulting both her and Jenny at the same time.

Then he asks Beatie why she isn't married yet, after three years of courting. How do you think Beatie feels when he asks that question? Do you get any hints from the stage directions here? What do you think Beatie really means by, 'We ent sure yit' (p. 103)? Who isn't sure – and why not?

Stan jokes that Beatie and Ronnie aren't sure how to make love; is he right?

Jenny firmly sends Stan off to bed, and he goes, after another sly dig at her for her weight. His last comment is about a new bridge they're building and you might like to wonder why Arnold Wesker included that comment. (p. 103)

Left alone, the three young people react in different ways. Jimmy dismisses the old man from his mind, saying he is ready for bed, and offering to let Beatie sleep in the soft bed rather than on the sofa, another indication of his basic kindness.

Beatie though cannot forget Stan Mann and his sickness; she talks of Ronnie's father, and the way Ronnie's mother looks after him. She is scared of having to look after an old person herself. What do you learn about Beatie from this – and about Ronnie from the comment of his she quotes?

Jimmy fetches his paper to go off to bed, suddenly noticing that the room is tidy. He neither approves nor disapproves, simply comments that it won't last, and disappears to bed.

This section of the scene shows very different reactions to the same thing by Jimmy and Beatie. What do their different reactions show you about them? (pp. 103–104)

Jenny gives Beatie a candle for light, and offers her a bedtime drink, which Beatie refuses. As they go off to bed, Beatie whispers loudly to Jenny that once she gets back to her parents, she'll bake some pastries for her sister. Jenny reminds her that Mr Bryant won't allow the expense, though Beatie argues with her. (Who is proved right in the end?)

Still whispering, as if they are two children talking after lights out, the sisters also discuss Beatie's paintings, which she says she'll show to Jenny. We get the impression that when they were younger Jenny and Beatie used to talk like this in bed at night.

They say good-night at last, and the stage darkens as the curtain falls.

This last section rounds off Beatie's visit to her sister's home. We learn a little more about her, her cooking, her painting, and we also are left, as the scene ends, with a homely feeling of life going on as usual.

Now that you have read the whole of the first act, you are in a position to take an overview of what is happening in the play.

You have met or heard about all the main characters. Make a list of them. Which have you actually seen, which only heard about? Include Ronnie in your list.

Now go through the list you've made, and jot down what you know about each character. Go back through the scene if you need to, to collect notes. Think about what you've learned of each person's personality, how they react to others, how others think about them. Ask yourself whether you like them, or what you've heard about them.

Also consider the ideas that Arnold Wesker is trying to explain to us in the play. What do you think is his main reason for writing *Roots* – to show us what? What does he have to say about such things as personal relationships – family life, romance, marriage? He certainly presents some very different, and often contrasting, views of these things; what are they? In the first act too, he has quite a lot to say about women, their place in society, their journey towards self-development. Of the female characters you've met, who do you think is more developed? Wesker presents his play against a background of poverty, and the fight for a political system which will combat poverty; what do you learn about these things in the first act?

Finally, ask yourself whether, in your view, the first act works. Maybe you have seen it performed, or maybe you have only read it. Whichever the case, consider the parts that make you interested or concerned, the sections which stir your emotions. If you find the play uninteresting, work out what it is about it that fails to appeal to you.

Before reading the second act of *Roots* ask yourself what you expect to happen next. Then read on and find out whether it does.

ACT 2, *Scene 1*

The time is two days later. Where has Beatie spent these two days? She is now on her way to her parents' home.

Once again the stage set is described, and it tells us about how Mr and Mrs Bryant live. As you did with Act 1, make sure you have a clear picture of what the stage looks like; draw a picture if it helps you. Have you included everything that is on the stage?

What do you find out from the description of the Bryants' cottage that helps you know what they are like as people? What is a 'tied' cottage – and what might this mean for the Bryants if Mr Bryant loses his job?

We also have a description of Mrs Bryant. As you did with other characters, write down five words of your own that tell you something about her. As you read more about her during the rest of the play, see if your initial impression of Mrs Bryant is the right one. Have you ever met anyone like Mrs Bryant; does she remind you of anyone you know?

As the scene opens, Mrs Bryant is calling the cat. She quickly loses patience with it, and starts peeling potatoes. Notice how, throughout the play, she never stops working. (p. 106)

Then Stan Mann comes in. He lives near Jenny and Jimmy; why then is he in this neighbourhood?

Read over the section where Stan and Mrs Bryant talk. Then choose from this list the phrases you think describe each of them. Write a paragraph about each character.

kindly
concerned
contented
frustrated with younger people
loves life
slightly disapproving
sad that the old days are gone
helpful
independent

How do the two older people get on together? Do they like each other, are they concerned for each other? Do they enjoy each other's company?

Notice in particular Stan Mann's comments about the younger generation. He feels that they don't really react to what is around them, but take their experience second-hand. They don't live life to the full, either. One of his comments is, '. . . long as they think it out theirselves' (p. 108). What does he mean by this?

That idea ought to remind you of someone else in the play, very different from Stan Mann, who feels the same. Who? In the end, Beatie herself comes to realize the wisdom of these ideas. In many ways, the ideal of thinking for oneself is the central point of the play. So why do you think Arnold Wesker chooses to have Stan Mann comment about it? (pp. 106–108)

Mrs Bryant is concerned about Stan's health (is she right to worry?) and packs him off home. Left to herself, she turns on the radio to loud dance music, so doesn't hear Beatie arriving.

What is the first thing Beatie does when she comes in? Notice how this typifies the difference between her and her mother.

Just as when Jenny and Beatie greet one another in Act 1, Mrs Bryant and Beatie say hallo in a reserved but affectionate way. Beatie is concerned about her things having arrived, they talk about which bus she came on, Beatie comments on having seen Stan Mann.

The conversation shows us, once again, quite a lot about Bryant family life. Complete these sentences about what it shows us:

Mrs Bryant's greeting to Beatie, 'Well, you've arrived then,' shows us . . .
Beatie's concern about her things coming shows us . . .
Mrs Bryant's comment, 'I hevn't touched a thing,' shows us . . .
Mrs Bryant's warning Beatie not to tell Pearl that she'd bought a gramophone shows us . . .
Beatie and Mrs Bryant talking about Stan Mann shows us . . .
Beatie's question, 'Got any tea Ma?' shows us . . .
Mrs Bryant's chatter about her flowers shows us . . .

Have you ever been away from home for a while? Has someone else in your family? What happened on the return home? Was the conversation like this? What would you expect Beatie and Mrs Bryant to talk about, after not seeing each other for a while? (pp. 108–109)

Next, the talk turns to Ronnie, and when he is coming to meet the family. Beatie warns Mrs Bryant to patch up the arguments she has had with Susan, her daughter, and Pearl, her daughter-in-law. Mrs

Bryant acts defensively, and is even more put out when Beatie asks her to put on a show for Ronnie when he arrives, not swearing, smartening the house up.

This issue of how Beatie wants her family to impress Ronnie runs throughout the play. At the very end, it is the reason why her mother turns on her. This is the first evidence of it that we see between Beatie and her mother, so look at it carefully.

Who do you sympathize with? Write down five sentences beginning with the words,

I sympathize with Beatie in this situation because . . .

and then five sentences beginning with the words,

I sympathize with Mrs Bryant in this situation because . . .

When you have completed both sets of sentences, decide which woman you sympathize with now. Then write a paragraph saying why.

This section of the scene also has Beatie quoting Ronnie once more, this time on the subject of what is right and what is wrong. What further impression do you get of Ronnie by what he is quoted as saying? Do you think, as Mrs Bryant does, that he sounds like a preacher? (pp. 110–11)

The scene moves on to a new section quite abruptly, as Beatie notices wasps in the room, and she and her mother begin a wasp hunt. Notice the difference in the way they are said, in the stage directions, to approach this. What does it show you about their characters?

Then Beatie says she wants to have a bath, so her mother fills up the copper (where she heats the water) from the water-tank in the garden.

Beatie meanwhile is unpacking, and telling her mother one of those odd, seemingly illogical dreams that people have. There are a few things to notice about this dream: first, the fact that Beatie dreams of dying, and that, a short while later, Stan Mann does in fact die.

What meanings could Beatie's dream have? Why do you think Arnold Wesker includes it in the play – to show us Beatie's character, her mother's character, to illustrate some theme in the play?

But even though this dream seems important to Beatie, her mother hardly listens. She is wrapped up in her own thoughts, about her day-to-day life, about the small dramas that go on in the village every day.

Beatie dreams about dying, while Mrs Bryant sees it happening around her.

Beatie hardly listens to her mother either, and is far more interested in showing her paintings. These are important to her. Why do you think this is? What does Ronnie say about them? How does Mrs Bryant react – and how do you think Beatie would have liked her to react? (pp. 111–13)

Next, as Beatie begins to bake a cake, she also starts to sing a folk-song. Mrs Bryant argues that a 'pop' song, 'I'll wait for you in the heavens blue', is far better, but Beatie says it is 'sloshy and sickly'. Spurred on by Ronnie's ideas about teaching people, Beatie tries to explain to her mother what is lacking in the pop song.

At first, Mrs Bryant won't listen; what is she far more interested in? But Beatie makes her listen, reciting the words of the song and inviting her mother to think about them. Beatie's point is that the words don't make her feel a particular way. Mrs Bryant can't tell the difference between that and opera songs, which don't make her feel particularly special, either.

Beatie recalls a row with Ronnie, over exactly the same things. Notice how she is annoyed with mother for not being able to understand, when she herself did not understand what Ronnie was saying. Read over the final paragraph on page 115 and see if you can understand what he is saying. What does Ronnie mean by:

'commercial world blunting our responses'.
'You can't learn how to live overnight.'
'we're still suffering from the shock of two world wars'.
'I'm going to make bloody sure I save someone from the fire'.

This section of the scene ends with Mrs Bryant again humming the pop song, and Beatie correcting her; Arnold Wesker comments that Beatie sings the song 'with some enthusiasm' to the end. What does this show you about Beatie?

In fact, at this point, Mrs Bryant says how good it is to have Beatie home; 'you do bring a little life with you anyway' (p. 116), and both women are surprised and a little embarrassed by her comment. Notice her final statement, 'The world don't want no feelings.' Is she right?

Have you ever had an argument with anyone over music? Has

anyone ever told you that the music you like is third-rate? What did they mean? How did you reply? Have you ever told someone else that the music they like is no good? What made you think that?

Songs, music are important in the play; look at this list of reasons, and choose the ones you think are nearest the truth.

Songs and music liven the play up.
Beatie's attitude to music shows us something about her.
Mrs Bryant's attitude to music shows us about her character.
Jenny's attitude to music shows us a lot about her.
Music and what it does for us is one of the main themes of the play.
The attitude to music of the working class is an important point in the play.
The attitude of the working class to all the arts is one of the play's messages.
The difference between good music and 'third-rate' music, explained in the play, shows us a lot about the best way to live.

Now write a paragraph on why music is important in the play; look for your evidence not only at this scene, but also at the end of Act 2 and Act 3. (pp. 113–16)

At this point Mr Bryant comes in. Notice the description of Mr Bryant, and the way he and Beatie greet each other, again with little emotion.

Mr Bryant is ill. The play seems to be full of the natural things of life, such as illness and death, which the country people take for granted. In fact, after a little conversation about his own pain, Mr Bryant tells the women that he has seen Stan Mann taken away in an ambulance.

Mr Bryant himself, though ill, waited with the old man while a friend went for help. All three characters express sympathy, and expect the old man not to live. But notice how, only a moment later, Beatie's father asks her which bus she came on.

The fact that Mr Bryant has left work is a serious matter. One of the sows is having a litter and he has to be there to see to her. Beatie, like a little girl, is keen to see the piglets.

Other pieces of news are exchanged – that Ronnie is coming to stay, that the family has to be on its best behaviour; Mr Bryant is rather put out at this.

This scene, where Beatie's father arrives home, once again shows us a lot about the characters as well as the messages of the play.

Choose the right answer to these questions:

1. The way Beatie and her father greet each other shows us that
   a. they do not consider showing emotion to be important.
   b. they do not feel anything for each other.
   c. Beatie's father is not feeling well.
   d. Mrs Bryant does not like to see them showing emotion.

2. The way Mr and Mrs Bryant talk to each other shows us all these
   things EXCEPT that
   a. Mr Bryant gets irritated with Mrs Bryant.
   b. Mrs Bryant is concerned that her husband may be ill.
   c. Mrs Bryant is worried that her husband may miss work.
   d. Mr Bryant wants to stay off work because he is lazy.

3. Mr Bryant's reaction to the news that Ronnie is coming shows us all
   these things EXCEPT that
   a. he is irritated that Beatie lives in London.
   b. he resents Ronnie.
   c. he doesn't want to be told not to swear.
   d. he really wants to meet Ronnie.

4. This particular scene gives us all these messages EXCEPT that
   a. Bryant family-life is quiet and undemonstrative.
   b. the working class are very dependent on work for survival.
   c. the Bryants' marriage is an example of how a good marriage can be.
   d. both Beatie and her mother are totally dependent.

(pp. 116–18)

At this moment Mr Healey arrives. He is Mr Bryant's boss. He's
described as polite, apologetic, but with a threat in his voice. What is
the threat; does it come true in the end?

Healey questions Mr Bryant about why he left work, and when
he'll be coming back. Does he need help? Read Mr Bryant's answers.
How do you think he says them? Choose some words from this list
that you think describe how he answers:

reassuringly	patronizingly
apologetically	anxiously
defiantly	hastily
submissively	confidently

Now write a paragraph about the way you think Mr Bryant feels during this part of the conversation with Healey.

What do you think of the way Healey handles the situation? Is he being tough on the old man, or is he just doing his job? How do you think he feels?

As he turns to go, Healey tells Mr Bryant that Stan Mann is dead. Bryant is amazed. Both men seem to take the news in their stride, as a natural part of life. (pp. 118–19)

When Mr Bryant tells the women the news about Stan Mann, they are shocked. Beatie in particular is quite tearful, although the older folk are able to criticize Stan as well as remember him fondly.

What do you feel about this reaction of the family to a death? Is it natural or hard-hearted? Whose reaction do you sympathize with most; Beatie's tearful reminiscences or the older folk's bewilderment that it should happen?

Why do you think Arnold Wesker has included a death, and at this point in the play? What message does it have for us, about the important themes in the play? What does it tell us about the characters, by the way they react to the news? (pp. 119–20)

The talk turns to Mr Healey; Mrs Bryant thinks he's a good sort, while Beatie thinks him threatening. She is angry at the way her father's job lies totally in Healey's hands. Notice how the Bryants feel powerless, Mr Bryant turning away from the union magazine, while Mrs Bryant is emphatic that nothing can be done. This should remind you of the section in Act 1 where Jimmy and Beatie talk about strikes. What, in general, is the country people's attitude to work and workers' power?

The poverty that their helplessness has landed them in is highlighted the next moment when Mr Bryant forbids Beatie to make a cake, saying that the electricity it uses is too expensive.

With whom do you sympathize here? Beatie is angry and upset, but does she realize the position her father is in? Mr Bryant is certainly worried about money, but is he also stingy?

In a broader sense, what do you learn about the Bryants' marriage? What does the way they handle money between them show you about their relationship as well as their individual characters?

From what Mrs Bryant says you can probably build up an idea of what their marriage is like on a day-to-day level, as well as the hopes she had at the beginning of their marriage. How do you think they felt about each other then – how do they feel about each other now?

Is there anything good to be seen in the Bryants' marriage? Can you find any part of it that makes it seem worthwhile? Would you like to be involved with a relationship like that?

Can you think of any ways that the Bryants could improve their relationship, or is it too late? Write a paragraph with your suggestions.

Think also of the way Mr Bryant treats Beatie; she is his daughter, but he still denies her things. How would you describe their relationship?

Notice how, at the end of the scene, Beatie chooses this moment to give her father the present she has bought for him. Why does Arnold Wesker have her give Mr Bryant the present now?

This section of the scene also tells us something about the place of women; what position is Mrs Bryant in, and can she do anything about it? Is Beatie any better off when she is dealing with her father; is she any better off when dealing with Ronnie? How much independence does she actually have?

The scene closes as Mrs Bryant suggests lunch; despite everything, the family is still hungry, as if to suggest that even when things are very serious, physical survival comes first. (pp. 120–122)

ACT 2, Scene 2

After lunch, the women are clearing up while Mr Bryant rolls himself a cigarette. Mr and Mrs Bryant are still not speaking to each other. Instead, they try to pass messages through Beatie, who will have none of it. Notice how, despite the quarrel, Mrs Bryant is concerned enough for her husband to want to choose the right thing for his tea.

Beatie wants to have her bath now. Mrs Bryant is concerned about the lack of privacy, so they decide to put curtains up; Mr Bryant tells Beatie that no one would want to see her naked. Again, be aware of the friendly teasing that goes on between them, even though a few minutes ago, they were arguing.

Mr Bryant gets Beatie's bath, her mother fetches the curtains, while Beatie lays her clothes out. (Even though the play is set only thirty years ago, there is no bath in the house.)

She is going to visit her brother Frankie and his wife Pearl. Do you remember anything about these two characters that we have been told in Act 1?

With a final exchange, via Beatie, about what to eat for tea, Mr Bryant goes off back to work.

This section, the beginning of Act 2, Scene 2, continues the quarrel begun in the previous scene. Now Mr and Mrs Bryant are showing their feelings about each other by not communicating, although you notice that they still cannot bear to keep silent. Talking through Beatie is merely a gesture. Have you ever known people quarrel by not speaking to each other? What is your opinion of that?

At the same time, in this section and the next, we see Beatie preparing for her bath. She has recovered very quickly from the row with her father; what does this show you about her character? (pp. 122–3)

In this section, Beatie takes her bath. She really enjoys both preparing it and having it. Read through the section, and note down the words, the expressions, and the stage directions that tell us that Beatie enjoys her bath. Why do you think Arnold Wesker has included Beatie's bath in the play; what does it show about her character, and that of her mother, what message does it have for us?

While Beatie is bathing, she and her mother talk. Mrs Bryant, as always, chatters on about village life, the people, the events. Beatie interrupts with her own affairs; Ronnie, his family, her bath. She and Mrs Bryant alternate with each other; do you think they actually listen to what the other is saying? Do you think that matters?

Mrs Bryant begins with Jimmy Skelton, arrested for accosting a man in the village; despite all this, Mrs Bryant still has good to say of him, and still continues to partner him at whist drives. What does this tell you about her character?

Beatie then talks about Ronnie's mother. You should by now be building up a picture, not only of Ronnie but of Ronnie's family. Ask yourself questions like these: do we know what they look like, do we know what their background is, do we know what their beliefs are, whether they are educated, rich, poor? Go through Beatie's comments in this scene, and in the other acts, and gather information about

Ronnie's family; what do you learn about Ronnie by doing this?

Beatie also comments about Ronnie, and the sort of life he lives, busy every moment. How does this compare with the way Beatie lives, and particularly with the way her family lives?

Then the conversation turns to food. Beatie wonders what they will feed Ronnie when he comes, and then comments that the reason many of the Bryant family have stomach ache is because country folk eat too much. It is certainly true that food plays a big part in the play. We see three meals being eaten or cleared away, and a great deal of baking and cooking too. Why do you think Arnold Wesker includes so many references to food in the play? What is he trying to tell us about country people?

While Beatie finishes her bath, Mrs Bryant continues gossiping, this time about an old woman she knew who went mad and was found in a tub of water up to her neck. It's ironic that while Mrs Bryant is telling this story, Beatie herself is up to her neck in water; the message here seems to be that some actions can be perfectly acceptable at some times, and prove a person mad when done in other ways. (pp. 124–6)

Now Beatie gets out of the bath. It is almost as if she has a new start to life. She stands in front of the mirror clothed in a bath towel, rubbing her hair, as if seeing her body for the first time; she listens to a slow, moving piece of classical music.

This moment, which comes at the emotional mid-point of the play, is important. Beatie is almost high, with an oddly clear vision of herself in all her glory, yet aware of the strangeness of being herself. She sees herself, wonders at herself, thinks for herself – all the things that Ronnie has been wanting her to do. Although she reverts to her old ways of behaving, this is the first inkling that she is breaking through to think for herself.

Notice how, just before this, she thinks about getting married, and thinks that when she is married, she'll be as happy as this every day. Is she right? If you were to meet Beatie, what would you say to her about marriage?

At the moment when Beatie is feeling elated at her discovery of herself, Mrs Bryant turns the radio off, stopping the beautiful classical music Beatie is enjoying.

Beatie turns on her mother, and they begin an argument which in many ways is at the centre of their relationship. Beatie complains that it is her mother's fault that she has not developed more, Mrs Bryant says that she had done all that a mother should do.

First, look at this list; which are the things Mrs Bryant accepts as part of a mother's job, and which are the things Beatie claims she should have done?

encourage a child to read
feed a child
allow the child to listen to classical music
concern oneself with what a child does
take a child out
be aware of what a child is learning
clothe a child

Which of these do you think a mother should do? Do you agree with Beatie that her mother didn't do her job – or with Mrs Bryant that it wasn't her responsibility to worry about how her daughter was developing? If it wasn't Mrs Bryant's responsibility, whose was it?

Beatie carries on ranting at her mother. She makes a series of points, all of them aimed at explaining to her mother what her dissatisfaction is. Answer these questions to make sure you understand what Beatie's points are.

1. Beatie talks about the holiday camp to make the point that
   a. town people and country people are no different.
   b. she hated working in a holiday camp.
   c. there was nothing interesting to write about in the camp.
   d. none of the girls there had the words to write about what happened.

2. Beatie talks about Ronnie's mother to make the point that
   a. some people care about their children.
   b. Ronnie's mother is an educated woman.
   c. her own mother doesn't care for her as much as Ronnie's mother did.
   d. Ronnie's mother and her own mother are very different.

3. Beatie talks about Stan Mann to make all these points EXCEPT
   a. Ronnie is really interested in people, even Stan Mann.
   b. Stan Mann's love of life would have appealed to Ronnie.
   c. Stan Mann should have been alive to talk to Ronnie.
   d. Ronnie would have accepted Stan Mann as an older person who couldn't change.

At one stage in Beatie's outburst, her mother comments that if Ronnie is trying to change people, he'll have a hard time with Beatie; and the girl replies that he is just trying to teach her and she is just trying to learn. Do you think she is right in her assessment of the situation? Is Ronnie trying to change her? Is she really trying to learn?

Finally, Beatie loses patience, sits her mother down and fetches the pick-up gramophone. She encourages her really to listen to *L'Arles-ienne*, a piece of music by Bizet. If you can, find a record of it, and listen to that piece yourself. (Notice though that Beatie herself admits to feeling resentful when Ronnie tries to get her to listen to music.)

She quotes Ronnie again, about Socialism, a political movement which aims at giving control into the hands of the working classes. He says that the movement is not just about talking, it is about doing the things that make life worthwhile, such as singing and dancing and asking questions.

At first it seems as if Mrs Bryant has not understood what Beatie is saying. Can you imagine what the old woman feels, after all Beatie's talk? But she does try to listen to the music that Beatie puts on the gramophone, and as Beatie gets more excited, so does her mother. The scene ends with them both smiling, clapping their hands, excited together and with the music.

What does this show, the fact that the scene ends with Beatie at last getting her mother to listen and respond to the classical music? Do you think Beatie is bringing her mother round to her point of view? Is she helping her to feel emotions? You might have one answer now, and another at the end of the play. (pp. 126–9)

ACT 3

Act 3 begins, as the others do, with a detailed description of the scene. It is set in the front room of Mrs Bryant's house, a room which, we guess, is opened only when visitors come. Read the description of the room and the furniture, and say what this tells us about the Bryants and how well-off they are.

The time is two weeks later, the day on which Ronnie is about to arrive. It's obvious that the Bryants have put on a spread for him, all the foods that they enjoy.

Notice too that Beatie has hung her paintings on the wall – what do you think she is aiming for in doing this? (pp. 130)

Beatie, who is upstairs changing, calls downstairs to her mother in the kitchen. How do you think they are each feeling at the moment? Write down a few notes about each of them. How do their feelings show in what they say to each other? (pp. 130–31)

Now Frankie, Beatie's brother, enters with his wife Pearl. We haven't met these two characters before, but have heard some things about them. Can you remember what?

Read through the description that Arnold Wesker gives of the two as they enter. What do you learn about each of them from this description?

Frankie calls to the family, wondering where they all are, and where Ronnie is. Beatie calls down that he hasn't arrived yet, and Frankie teasingly queries the fact that Ronnie is a socialist, and Jewish; he can't understand Beatie for being attracted to someone like that. Frankie is amazed that Ronnie hasn't written yet, though Pearl realizes that mentioning it will only embarrass Beatie. (That Ronnie hasn't been in touch is in fact significant; can you remember why?)

Beatie comes down, dressed in her new frock. She is looking happy; why do you think this is? She greets Frankie and Pearl, and they start talking about the rest of the family, and their quarrels. Pearl complains about Mrs Bryant's behaviour, and Frankie comments that Mrs Bryant and her mother haven't spoken since the mother took Jenny in when she had an illegitimate child.

Notice the relationship between Beatie and the family. How would you describe it – intense, friendly, hostile? As the rest of the family come in, start building up a representation of how the Bryant family get on together. What sort of people are they? How do they treat each other? How, in particular, do husbands and wives react together? Does Beatie join in, or is she apart from all this? (pp. 131–3)

Now Jimmy and Jenny come in, and there are more casual greetings. Frankie asks Jimmy whether he has yet formed the association he was talking about when they were all having a drink one night. Without a shadow of embarrassment, Frankie explains that Jimmy was feeling sexually frustrated, and suggested that men and women who felt like that should have a system — a badge and a password perhaps — for recognizing each other.

Jimmy is really embarrassed; what do you think he is afraid of, and from whom? But Frankie carries on, describing how a possible meeting might be arranged. When he has finished there is a long silence, and you might be tempted to think that Jenny in particular is embarrassed or upset. In fact, she retorts with a suggestion that maybe the women in that situation might want more sex than a man.

Why do you think Arnold Wesker includes this incident in the play? What does it show about the people involved, their relationships and their attitudes to sex? Is he making any point about the place of sex in a relationship or a marriage? (pp. 131–4)

After this interlude, the talk turns to Ronnie again. Of course, everyone is curious to know what he's like, though the family as a whole seem to think that, from what Beatie has said, he is rather strange. We also learn a little more about Ronnie's family.

Notice how many warnings Beatie gets from her family about Ronnie. You might like, at some point, to list the characters, and then check through the play to find out which of them expresses doubt about Ronnie and his relationship with Beatie. She consistently defends him. In the end, who is proved right? (p. 134)

At this point, Mr Bryant comes in. Now all the family except for Stan and Susie are present. (Why do you think Arnold Wesker does not include them in the family party?)

Beatie immediately rushes her father to get changed, and at first, so does Mrs Bryant, until she realizes that her husband is upset. At first he says there is nothing the matter, but then admits that he has been put on casual labour.

This is a much more serious matter than it seems. What does it actually mean for the Bryants in terms of their standard of living? Why has Healey done this to Bryant — and what does it show about Healey as a person? In fact, this is the worst possible time Bryant could have been put on half-pay, just when he is feeling ill.

How do the family react, in their different ways? Link the characters listed below to the reactions also listed.

Mrs Bryant	gets upset and angry.
Beatie	is philosophical, calm.
Frankie	looks after Mr Bryant in a practical way.
Jenny	
Jimmy	

Notice how none of the family actually sympathize directly with Mr Bryant – it is not their way. He himself is depressed but accepts the change; he has probably expected it for a while, and this may be why he has been so tight with money.

What is your judgement on the way the following people act; write a few sentences about each, saying how they act and whether or not you agree with the way they act: Healey, Beatie, Mrs Bryant, the rest of the family. Would you say that Mrs Bryant's words show her to be a supportive wife, or that Beatie's reactions show anything about the difference between her and the rest of the family?

Also, look at what the whole of this incident shows us about the place of people like the Bryants in society. Because they are poor and lower-class, they are vulnerable, and can easily be affected by the decisions of those who employ them. What message do you think Arnold Wesker has for us here? What do you think Ronnie would have had to say about what happens – and do you think Beatie's reactions are affected by all the things about society that she has heard Ronnie say? (pp. 134–5)

When Mr Bryant goes up to change, the family sits in a companionable silence. The talk turns to Stan Mann's companion (not wife; we discover that they were not married) who is feeling quite low now that he has died. Although they were not married, she has obviously been devoted to him, moving in after his first stroke and staying to look after him, despite the fact that she lost her job because of it.

How do the family react to this? They seem to be sympathetic, not condemning the pair for living together. Compare this with other actions in the play that various characters react to:

Jenny having an illegitimate baby.
Beatie living with Ronnie.
Stan Mann messing himself.
Pearl quarrelling with Mrs Bryant.
Jimmy suggesting a 'sexual frustration' club.

Jimmy Skelton accosting a man.
Mr Bryant losing his job.
Stan Mann's death.

What is your opinion of each of these events? Some may seem to you
shocking, others trivial; think about each and decide what you think
about it. Then consider how people in the play think about each,
whether they are shocked or not. In particular, consider how Mrs
Bryant reacts to each, how Beatie reacts to each. What does this show
you about values in the Bryant family, and how Beatie holds the
same, or different, values?

After a few casual comments between the members of the family,
Mrs Bryant comes in, having put the kettle on. (pp.136–7)

The question of what is an action that shocks and what is a socially
acceptable action is continued into the next section of the play.

Among the chatter Mrs Bryant hears that a boy convicted of assault
got six years in prison. She is very angry, reacting strongly to this
threat to law and order.

Beatie, half amused, half angry herself, challenges her mother to
pass judgement on the boy; to show some understanding of the
situation before simply passing a life sentence. Mrs Bryant has
no logical backing for her anger, and Beatie triumphantly calls
her bluff. She complains that the family in general never thinks
things through, never discusses matters – such as Mr Bryant's loss of
job.

Beatie and her mother are on the point of an argument over all this
when Mr Bryant comes down, now dressed in his work clothes, and
Mrs Bryant goes to make the tea. The family turns back to gossiping
again, much to Beatie's frustration.

This scene is the next step to Beatie's real disillusionment with her
family and the way they approach life. She has seen them react
passively to Mr Bryant's redundancy; now she sees that none of them
really think issues through, they just pass judgement. When she
challenges her mother, Mrs Bryant doesn't even seem to understand
what the girl is talking about.

What else are you learning about the family, and Beatie's place in
it? Would you like to be part of the Bryant family, or do you see ways
in which they behave that would make you angry too? Is there

anything about the way they face life that reminds you of the way the members of your family act? (pp. 137–8)

Mrs Bryant enters with the tea, and Beatie, tired of the small talk, tells the family she is going to set them a problem.

What do you think her reasons for doing this are; choose the ones from this list that you think are most likely, and write a paragraph about Beatie's reasons, and whether you agree with them. She tells it

to amuse the family while they wait for Ronnie.
to shock the family.
to show her mother that she never thinks about things.
to show the whole family that they never talk deeply.
to show her independence.
to give the family an opportunity to think and talk deeply.

Now Beatie tells her story. List the following parts of it in the correct order, to show that you know the story.

a. The girl hears that Archie is going to America.
b. A girl lives on one side of the stream.
c. He agrees if she travels across naked.
d. She goes to Archie's hut and declares her love for him.
e. On the other side live Archie and Tom.
f. The girl loves Archie, but he doesn't love her.
g. When he hears the story, he chucks her out.
h. The girl wants the ferryman to take her across the river.
i. The ferryman takes the girl across the stream.
j, A wise man lives on the same side of the stream.
k. He says he loves her and she spends the night with him.
l. She goes to Tom and asks for his help.
m. Tom loves the girl but the girl doesn't love Tom.
n. He says to do what she thinks best.
o. In the morning, Archie has left her.
p. The girl asks the wise man for advice.

Beatie asks the family who they think is to blame for the girl's problem. Before you begin to consider their answers, think about the problem for yourself. Who do you think is to blame?

Now make a list of the characters in this scene: Mr Bryant, Mrs Bryant, Jimmy, Jenny, Pearl, Frankie, Beatie. Read through the passage from pp. 140–41, where they express their opinions, and write down opposite each name the opinions the person expresses.

What do you learn about each character from the way they react to this story? Who do you think reacts best, who in the way you least admire?

Does Beatie get what she wants from the incident – or not? And in fact, is she herself doing what she wants the family to do, thinking independently?

What else, apart from showing us about the characters in the play, do you think Arnold Wesker is telling us by introducing this moral dilemma? What messages does the whole incident contain? At any rate, this moral dilemma not only starts us thinking about what is right and wrong, but builds up the emotion – as Beatie becomes more and more animated – for the scene to follow.

Beatie begins to quote Ronnie, standing on a chair and thrusting her fist in the air. She is excited, not only at challenging the family, but also at the thought of Ronnie's imminent appearance. She quotes him over and over again, on morals, how to behave, politics. What does this show about the way she feels about him – and also about how much (or how little) she herself has developed as a person?

At the end of her tirade, there is a knock at the door. (pp. 138–42) Beatie jumps down from her chair to open the door; she thinks it is Ronnie arriving, and shouts 'He's here, he's here!'

It is the postman, bringing a letter for Beatie and a parcel for mother, her dress from the club, which immediately leads to an argument between her and Pearl. Against this background, Beatie is reading her letter, and it immediately becomes obvious that she is stunned by what she is reading.

So it is Mrs Bryant who takes the letter and reads it out to the family. (Why do you think Arnold Wesker has Mrs Bryant, an unsympathetic person, read the letter out and not Beatie?)

The letter is from Ronnie, the first and only time in the play we hear him speaking for himself. His first words are 'It wouldn't really work would it?' and the rest of the letter explains his reason for wishing to end the relationship.

Read the letter again, then make a list of the reasons Ronnie gives. Do you think he really means it, that he is sincere in wanting to split up? Do you agree with his reasons?

From reading his words, what impression do you form of Ronnie and his personality? Also, what do you learn about Beatie, and her way of handling the relationship with Ronnie, from this letter? Does it fit in with the impression of the relationship that she has been giving during the play?

Did you, when you first read the play, expect Ronnie to end the relationship – was it a surprise to you that Arnold Wesker makes this happen? Do you think it is a good thing to happen, or that it adds to the play?

As Mrs Bryant reads the letter, Beatie becomes more and more upset; eventually she snatches the letter from her mother, and replies angrily to her father's question about whether Ronnie is coming or not.

How do you imagine Beatie is feeling throughout this section of the play; make a list of words that you think might describe her state, and then write a paragraph, as if you were Beatie, describing your very first reactions when you got the letter. (p. 142)

Now the family begins to become involved. Mrs Bryant immediately reacts with anger towards Beatie, while Jenny questions her sister as to whether she expected the relationship to break up.

Beatie slowly begins to realize that the ways she has not been able to keep up with Ronnie have in fact destroyed the relationship.

Read through the section on pages 143–4 where Beatie, slowly growing more hysterical, realizes the ways she has not listened to Ronnie, not met what he expected of her. How many ways does she list? Do you think her not doing these things has really affected the way she and Ronnie relate? Do you think she is to blame for the relationship splitting up?

Then, unable to take the burden of feeling that it is all her fault, Beatie turns on her family. She accuses the Bryants of sitting by while she messed up her relationship, of bringing her up in a way that blocked her from really being able to keep Ronnie. Do you think Beatie is right in blaming her family?

Certainly, Mrs Bryant does not think she is to blame; she has little time for Beatie's anger, believing that she has done all she can by holding a family party. Do you agree with her? (pp. 144–5)

In the end, driven to distraction by Beatie's near-hysteria, Mrs Bryant slaps Beatie's face, to everyone's shock.

She then expresses her point of view. Read Mrs Bryant's speech on pages 144–5, and make sure you really understand it. What is she saying? Choose from this list the statements that reflect Mrs Bryant's point of view.

Mrs Bryant feels

that she's had enough of Beatie telling her what to do.
that Beatie is part of the family.
that Beatie is blaming her for the faults Beatie herself has.
that Beatie herself is stubborn, does not understand, makes no effort.
that she likes being responsible for Beatie.
that she would prefer to leave, but she knows there are people who depend on her.
that Beatie has spent two weeks telling her that she's a fool.
that Beatie can fend for herself, seeing as she thinks so badly of her mother.

By the end of Mrs Bryant's tirade, Beatie has begun to agree with her; do you think her agreement is genuine or is she just trying to keep the peace?

Mrs Bryant, however, is not pacified. She keeps on at Beatie, saying, 'I suppose he weren't satisfied wi' goodness only.' What do you think she means by this – what judgement is she passing on Ronnie, and on his attitude to Beatie? Do you agree with her?

What do you learn about Mrs Bryant from this section of the play? Is it the first time she has really spoken out about her view, her opinion of Beatie and the way she treats the family? Does it increase your respect for Mrs Bryant or not? Do you see her any differently when she talks about what she would do if she were free?

What does it show you, too, about the Bryant family ties? Are they natural; does Mrs Bryant resent what she has had to do for her family?

And what insights do you get about Beatie? Do you agree with her mother that when Beatie attacks Mrs Bryant, she is in fact talking about her own faults? (pp. 144–5)

Mrs Bryant finally, angry with Beatie for not responding, invites her to, 'Talk – go on, talk.'

But at first, Beatie seems to accept that she too is like the rest of the Bryant family, unable really to talk about what she feels in a real and direct way. Despairingly, Beatie says she cannot talk. Nevertheless, she begins to express herself, at first slowly, about the lack of 'roots' in her life.

What does Beatie mean by 'roots', the word she introduces here, and which is the title of the play? Read over the speeches on pages 145–6 where she explains what she means, and see if you can then put her definition of 'roots' into your own words. What does she mean?

Mrs Bryant thinks Beatie means the family, but this is not what Beatie is thinking of. Pearl cannot understand her, but Beatie carries on seeming, slowly and surely, to find her words.

She turns on the family, now challenging them to show any signs of real life, of real connectedness to what is going on around them. She quotes her sister, saying that life meant so little to her that she would not care if the bomb dropped.

When Mrs Bryant refers to radio and television as ways to stave off boredom, Beatie points out that these are all ways of entertainment that demand no effort, no response, no real thought. Do you agree with her? Do you think the ways you find to entertain yourself make you think? No one nowadays, Beatie says, asks questions, wonders about anything, fights for anything. And it is our own fault – so Ronnie says.

Both Jimmy and Mrs Bryant react defensively to this, saying that if that is all Ronnie thought about them, they are pleased not to have met him. But Beatie realizes that Ronnie would, in fact, have defended the country people, for he had some idea (about which Beatie is mocking) that their lives, so close to nature, are in some way more valuable. Beatie however says that the sort of people her family are, the workers, are not really important, because they make no effort to appreciate quality, in art or in life. So they condemn themselves to being, and receiving, second-rate culture.

This is a new idea, and you may be becoming aware that Beatie is slowly developing ideas of her own. What does this show about her?

Do you agree with her new ideas? Do you think that the workers are satisfied with a culture (art, music, films, books, magazines, the theatre) that are just second-rate – and so that's what they get?

Beatie also links this in with money. The workers have the money, so the people who produce films and magazines are eager to please them, and to give them what they want; and what they want, she repeats, is low-quality entertainment. She feels patronized and insulted by this.

In the middle of her tirade, Beatie stops. She has suddenly realized that she is, for the first time in her life, speaking for herself. She has, in fact, contradicted her belief that she cannot think or speak on her account – and by speaking so emotionally and about real issues, has also contradicted her own argument that the working classes show only second-rate things.

But the Bryant family do not realize what is happening. They cannot see the change in Beatie; they go off and have their tea.

Beatie however, as the play ends, seems to have a revelation; as if she hears herself for the first time, liking what she hears, she begins to speak, calling on Ronnie, on God, to witness that she is beginning to think and speak as a woman alone.

This final scene is the climax of the play. In it we see Beatie changing, and we also realize that her family will never change. (pp. 145–8)

You may have realized that in fact, it is Ronnie's ending the relationship that makes Beatie, for the first time, think for herself. At the very point where everyone rejects her, when she is not depending on family or boyfriend for support, she finds she can stand alone.

How do you feel about Beatie at the end of the play? Do you see her differently now from the way you did at the beginning? Do you feel with her as she changes her way of looking at the world?

What about the Bryant family? What do you think of them for the way they react to Beatie when she gets the news, when she makes her realizations? Do you despise or sympathize with them? In particular, how does your view of Mrs Bryant change?

And what do you feel Arnold Wesker is trying to tell us about life during this last section of the play? What are his messages about family life, and the relationships in the family? What does he have to say about love and the way people affect each other when they relate in that way? How does he represent women in particular, in love and out of it, finding their independence and their place in life?

Perhaps most importantly, what does he have to say about the working class, and its place in society, its level of thought and feeling? Do you think he agrees with what Beatie says?

Final questions to consider, as you think back on the play, are these: does the last scene leave you feeling elated, or depressed, hopeful, or hopeless about the world? And what have you learned about yourself, and your life, from watching Beatie and her life change?

For if reading, or watching, a play like *Roots* changes your view of the world, then even though it was written thirty years ago, about issues that were real thirty years ago, it remains a play that is relevant, and valuable, today.

Characters

HEALEY

One of the few characters we meet in the play who is not really part of the Bryant family is Mr Healey, Bryant's boss. He appears in Act 2, Scene 1, for a brief interchange with Mr Bryant about the fact that he went home through illness, and also gives the news of Stan Mann's death. We do not see him again, but hear of him when Bryant loses his steady employment in Act 3.

Why do you think Healey is included in the play? His character is not developed, and we learn very little about him. His usefulness seems to be to represent the outside world, and also a different, higher class than the Bryants. Unlike Ronnie, however, who is also of a different class, he seems to have little sympathy with the workers. As soon as Mr Bryant is unable to work, he puts him on to casual labour.

Healey is also useful by showing us more about the other characters. The way the Bryants, and Beatie, react to him shows us how they view authority and the class system – and in particular how the sacking affects Beatie. Though a very minor character then, Healey does have a contribution to make to the play.

PEARL

Pearl is Beatie's sister-in-law, and we meet her briefly in Act 3, having heard something about her in the first Act. What sort of person is she? She seems attractive, but ordinary, with few original thoughts of her own, and a stubborn, quarrelsome nature. Beatie certainly does not think too much of her, stating that she wasn't good enough to be marrying Frank.

The quarrel between Pearl and Mrs Bryant is the subject of gossip throughout the play; why do you think Arnold Wesker includes it? Pearl, just as much as the rest of the Bryant family, is only reacting to what is around her – a quarrel with her mother-in-law is literally one of the most dramatic things in her life, and from that we learn quite a lot about family life, and about what Beatie sees as the life of the working class.

We also learn from Pearl another view of what it is like to be a woman, to contrast with those presented by Beatie, Mrs Bryant and Jenny. She has little to say for herself, little to say to Frankie, and her only really strong emotion comes when she blames the girl in Beatie's story, showing little understanding or sympathy for her.

We have mentioned some of the ways in which Pearl contributes to the play. Can you think of any more?

FRANKIE

Frankie, Beatie's brother, is another character whom we only meet briefly in the play – in Act 3. Beatie mentions him in the first act, and we do learn some things about him then, that Beatie considers him to have made an unworthy marriage, that when they were children, she and Frankie quarrelled.

In Act 3, Frankie appears on stage. Read the description of him on page 131, and then the times he speaks during the rest of the act. What do you learn about him? Read these statements, and, for each, comment on it and say how true you think it is.

Frankie is shy.
He is not afraid of criticizing his mother.
He likes jokes, even if they embarrass people.
He treats everything as a joke.
He is slightly cynical about the Bryant family.
When Beatie gets the letter, Frank has no idea how to respond.
He is emotional and romantic.
He is concerned about Beatie and her happiness.

He is suspicious of Ronnie.
He hates being part of the Bryant family.

What picture of Frankie do you form from what you learn about him? Do you sympathize with or like him? Look particularly at the point where he defends the girl who is ruined; this can be seen as Frankie at his best; does the incident make you feel differently about him, or understand him better?

Why do you think Arnold Wesker includes Frankie in the play? Is it just that Beatie needs to have a brother in the family? What does he add to the play by being there? Make a list of things that Frankie adds, and for each, give an example from what he says or does to illustrate your point.

STAN MANN

Stan Mann is not one of the Bryants, but he is of their class, and he is a friend. We hear about him, as a farmer who has come down in the world; then we see him, a sad old man who has just messed himself. Later in the play, his death affects all the Bryants.

Stan is a sad character. He reminds us of how things will be for the Bryants when Mr Bryant is not working. He shows us what happens in people's old age. He warns us against drunkenness.

But in some ways he is a hopeful character. Do you find anything to like about him? At his age, he is still frisky, flirting with Mrs Bryant and Beatie. He is also clear-sighted, talking shrewdly about Beatie's relationship even though he knows very little about it, and commenting wisely on young people today. Look at his comment on pages 107–8, about what happens to people when they stop reacting to life and thinking for themselves. For all that Beatie criticizes the lower class country folk, Stan Mann is very wise.

How does his death affect the family? And what do we find out about Stan in their talk about him? What does it show about him that, even after his first stroke, he attracted someone so much that she came to live with him?

At the end of the play, Stan seems to be forgotten. But what things does he say and do which in fact add to our understanding of what happens at the end of the play? Notice too that he is the only character in the book, apart from Beatie and Ronnie, to talk about building 'bridges'.

JIMMY

Jimmy is Beatie's brother-in-law. We get to know quite a bit about him in the first act, though we see him only briefly after that.

What is Jimmy like? Make a list of what you have learned about him from reading the play. Use these headings to gather your notes:

what he looks like
how he speaks
what things are important to him in life
how he thinks of his work
how he thinks of his wife
how he relates to Beatie
what personality he has
what you don't like about him
what you like about him

If you have seen *Roots* performed, be careful not to confuse the play as Arnold Wesker wrote it with the performance you saw.

Now use your notes to write a character description of Jimmy, including all these points. Remember to include proof of the points you are making by referring to incidents in the play, things people say and do, quotations from the play.

Now think about Jimmy's role in the play. What is he there for? Do you think his character is interesting? Does it, by contrasting with any other character, show you more about both people in the play? Does Jimmy show us more about Beatie, for example, by the way she relates to him?

Certainly Jimmy shows us more about the ideas that Arnold Wesker is writing about. He is one of the married men in the play, and shows us one aspect of what it is like to be married and to have a family. Do you think he loves Jenny – why do you think he married her when she already had a baby by someone else? And what does it show you about Jimmy that, in Act 3, we hear how he wants a club for the sexually frustrated?

Imagine you are Jimmy. Think about your life in Norfolk with Jenny, Daphne and the Bryant family. How do you feel about your life? Write a paragraph explaining whether you are happy or not. Then write a paragraph about the party in Act 3, giving your view about what happened, and how you feel about Beatie.

MR BRYANT

Mr Bryant, Beatie's father, seems in some ways an unsympathetic figure. Tight with money, dominant with his family, he just doesn't seem to understand his wife or children.

What impression do you get of him when you read the play? He is described as a 'small, shrivelled man', he is physically weak, he works as a farm labourer. And what do you learn about his character? Read this list of personality traits, and then comment on which you think apply to Mr Bryant.

outgoing	intelligent
confident	educated
stubborn	emotional
hard-working	sympathetic
caring	anxious

We probably learn most about him when we see him relating to other people. Complete these sentences with statements about how Mr Bryant interacts with the rest of his family and those about him.

When he is with . . . he . . .

his wife
Mr Healey
Beatie
Stan Mann

One of the major things to notice here is what Mr Bryant's relationship with his wife shows us about love, marriage and family life. What sort of marriage do they seem to have? Do you think they still love each other? Find some words and actions in the play that suggest that they don't – and then some that suggest that they do. Is theirs a relationship that you admire, or would like to be part of? When you think about what is wrong with the relationship, how far do you think Mr Bryant is to blame?

Perhaps the point in the play where Mr Bryant is most important is where he comes home with the news that he has lost his regular job. We see Mr Bryant depressed and withdrawn, and for a moment the whole action of the play revolves around him. We learn that the family reacts with very little emotion to the shattering news, so much so that Beatie is appalled. We also realize what effect it has on poor country people when employment is withdrawn, a real-life example of the class problems that Ronnie has merely been talking about. We begin to realize just why Mr Bryant has been so tight with money.

At the end of the play, when Beatie first challenges the family with a puzzle, and then is herself stopped short by Ronnie's letter, Mr Bryant is lost. He literally doesn't understand what is going on, and in the final moments of the play says nothing. Why do you think this is? Is he being awkward – or is the whole thing just out of his experience?

You should be able to see, then, that even though Mr Bryant is not a sympathetic character at first sight, he is nevertheless very important to the play. We learn about other characters through him, and his actions and what happens to him show us a lot about relationships and class problems. You may still, though, have difficulty liking him – do you?

JENNY

Jenny is Beatie's sister. Begin by finding out what she looks like, and imagining her in your mind. You'll find a full description of her in Act 1. There too you'll find a description of her house, which will tell you something about Jenny herself.

What is she like as a person? She seems placid, satisfied with her life, untidy, but a good cook. We find little touches of humour, little flashes of temper, but in general she is a sensible, down-to-earth country-woman.

How does she react to the people around her? Her main relationship is with Jimmy, her husband. Does she care for him, look after him? Do you think she loves him – and what does she say when Beatie asks her the same question? She certainly seems to have a stable marriage, and to be happy with it. She is tolerant of Jimmy's 'sexual frustration' club, even though she is shocked when Beatie talks about making love, and she and Jimmy plan to have children some day. She herself has already had a child, and you can discover a lot about Jenny by thinking about this fact, and about the way she calmly and effectively had the child, without telling anyone who the father is, and then married Jimmy.

What about Jenny's attitude to her mother? How would you describe this? She sees her mother very realistically, but does not condemn her as Beatie does. And she is tolerant too about the other members of the family, and the quarrels they have.

Jenny and Beatie are in some ways very similar, and in some ways very different. Jenny seems fond of her sister; they get on well in Act 1, and in Act 3 she defends her against Mrs Bryant's anger, and is genuinely sorry when Beatie gets the letter. On the other hand, Jenny sometimes seems frustrated with Beatie's attitudes and opinions, and she certainly feels that her sister is making a mistake about the relationship with Ronnie – and she is right.

Fill in this list, comparing and contrasting Jenny and Beatie. One of the reasons Jenny is in the play is to help us understand Beatie more, and provide a different point of view from Beatie's.

Jenny is like Beatie in background in that . . .
Jenny and Beatie have both . . .
Jenny and Beatie are both . . .
Jenny sympathizes with Beatie because . . .
Jenny, unlike Beatie, has . . .
Jenny, unlike Beatie, is . . .
Jenny thinks differently from Beatie about . . .
Jenny feels differently from Beatie about . . .

Another reason for Jenny's presence is to show us certain things about key ideas in the play. What do you think she has to say to us about love, what it is and how it is important? Are her ideas of love the same as Beatie's? Who is right? What about marriage, family life, and sexuality? What messages does Jenny have for us about these topics?

In particular, Jenny shows us something about the life of women. She, her mother and Beatie are very different, but together they present a fuller picture of what a woman is, and can be. What particular strengths does Jenny have that neither Mrs Bryant nor Beatie shows?

To gather together all the ideas you've gained about Jenny, write a paragraph or two about her place in the play, and why it is important.

MRS BRYANT

The two most important people in Beatie's life are Ronnie and her mother. Mrs Bryant is a memorable character, in some ways likeable, and in some ways most unsympathetic.

Find out from Act 2 what she looks like, and get a clear picture of her in your mind, imagining how she would move, what her voice would sound like. Then begin to add to this picture. Ask yourself questions like these about Mrs Bryant, and answer them from your knowledge of the play. If you can't answer them right away, read back over the play until you can.

What is Mrs Bryant's background?
Is she rich or poor?
Is she clever, knowledgeable, educated?
Is she a good housewife?
How does she get on with other people – her family, her friends?
What does she like?
What does she ignore or dislike?
What is important to her about life?

By this time, you should have a clearer understanding of Mrs Bryant, and be ready to consider her character in more depth. Start, first of all, by considering how Mrs Bryant relates to other people.

What is her relationship with her husband like? If you were a marriage-guidance counsellor, what advice would you give the Bryants – to stay together, or to separate? Do you think they would want your advice? Consider what Mrs Bryant, her words and actions show us about marriage, its problems and rewards – and also what they show us about love.

What is her relationship with her children like? Do you think she brought them up well? During the play, there is a lot said about what a mother's duties are, and you might like to think again about what you think they are, and how far Mrs Bryant fulfils them. Certainly her relationship with her children has changed now they are adult. Notice how, for most of the Bryant family, quarrels (particularly not speaking) are a regular way of life. Mrs Bryant has also stopped speaking to her own mother, because the old lady took Jenny in when she was pregnant!

We do see Mrs Bryant relating to other people. She is kind to Stan Mann, deferential to Healey. She tells us about meeting others, seeming not to mind that her regular cards partner has been had up for accosting men, seeming to be genuinely sad about the neighbour who went mad.

In particular, though, look at Mrs Bryant's relationship with Beatie. Does she love her daughter? There is certainly a reserved affection between them, and she brings water, cooks, hangs Beatie's pictures.

It is interesting too to compare and contrast the two women. How is Mrs Bryant like Beatie? How different? How far is Beatie her mother's daughter – and do you think she will grow to be like her mother when she is older?

At the end of the play however, when Beatie needs her mother, Mrs Bryant is resentful and angry. Read this last scene carefully, asking yourself whether there is any truth in what Mrs Bryant says about Beatie. Is she being vicious, or far-sighted? Is there any truth in what Beatie says about her mother? And do you sympathize with Mrs Bryant's words and actions? Should she have spoken and acted differently?

This last scene, as well as making us ask questions about the two women's points of view, shows us clearly the difference between them. Like Jenny, Mrs Bryant's role in the play is partly to act as a contrast to Beatie. List the ways in which they are the same, and the ways in which you feel they are different. Do you think Beatie will, one day, grow to be a woman like her mother?

Finally then, consider what Mrs Bryant shows us about being a woman. She is a very particular sort of woman, different from Beatie and Jenny in many ways, but nevertheless with her own strengths and virtues. Do you think Arnold Wesker wants us to like her, sympathize with her? And do you, in fact, warm to Mrs Bryant as a character?

RONNIE

Although Ronnie never once appears on stage, he is nevertheless one of the most vital characters in *Roots*. We never see him, have no physical description of him, but through Beatie's eyes, and through her words, we get a clear picture of him. He influences the play in a number of ways, and in the end, is responsible for Beatie's leap into self-development.

What do we in fact learn about Ronnie, even though we do not even know what he looks like? If you have the time, go through the play, marking each place where he is mentioned or, more especially, where Beatie quotes his exact words. Read these extracts through, and begin to build up a representation of this person who so influences the play. He is Jewish, he comes from an educated family, he loves talking, writing, anything that involves words. He is full of ideas about the class struggle, politics, relationships, morals, justice, art, music.

Make a list of all the things that Ronnie has ideas about; use the list above as a starting point. Then once you have read 'his' speeches, make notes under each heading on what Ronnie's ideas really are. What does he believe about all these things?

By this time, you should be gaining some opinion about Ronnie. What do you feel about him – would you like him if you met him, or do you feel that he just talks for the sake of talking?

Beatie herself has a number of attitudes towards Ronnie. Which of these words describe the way she feels about him? When you have chosen the ones you think best fit, write a paragraph, as if you were Beatie at the start of the play, saying how you feel about Ronnie.

Beatie . . . admires, loves, respects, adores, hates, resents, fears, is in awe of, enjoys, fancies, is infatuated with, is committed to, wants to help, wants to marry, is insecure with . . . Ronnie.

Beatie certainly wants her family to like Ronnie. She spends a great deal of the play telling them about him, and encouraging them to prepare for his visit. She is concerned in case he is not impressed by them, and therefore does not like her.

How do they feel about him? In general, they dislike the sound of him, and are suspicious and defensive. Their reaction ranges from joking sarcasm from Frankie to serious worry from Jenny, to final anger from Mrs Bryant. Even Stan Mann is concerned that they haven't married yet. However they all do their best to prepare for him, and welcome him when he comes.

And when he doesn't come, all the family are horrified, though some of them are not surprised. Mrs Bryant turns on Beatie, and frankly points out Ronnie's faults, and they all declare that they would not have liked him anyway. After a short while they forget the problem.

Beatie of course, cannot forget, but because of Ronnie's action in jilting her, she gains something she would not otherwise have gained – self-development. Ronnie's letter (read it over again) may seem suspect. You may feel that he is worming his way out of a relationship that no longer satisfies him – or you may feel he is escaping from a partnership that did not give him what he wanted. Does it seem to you that Ronnie acted well in the relationship itself – or did he just use Beatie, and then reject her?

You may ask yourself if you blame Ronnie for finishing with Beatie, or if you sympathize with him. But at any rate, he does Beatie a favour. He allows her, for the first time, to start thinking for herself.

It's possible that having the relationship with Ronnie was the best thing that ever happened to Beatie – except finishing the relationship, which spurs her on even more. So in this way, he is vitally important to the play. His ideas – about love, sex, marriage, the class struggle – show us very clearly some of the ideas Wesker values (and some that he criticizes). His character, on its own and contrasting with others in the play, adds to our understanding of these ideas. In these three ways, Ronnie is seen as a vital character.

That said, it may be that you find him unappealing as a character. Have you ever known anybody like him? Did you like them? Ask yourself again, having studied the play, the question we encouraged you to ask when you first read about Ronnie; do you think you would like him if you met him?

BEATIE

Beatie is, of course, the heroine of *Roots*. The play is the story of a major event in her life, which changes her and her view of the world. She is actually the only character in the play who is seen to change (apart from Ronnie, who changes his mind), and this shows that she is the most developed, and most valuable person in it.

Beatie is blonde and well-built; she enjoys her own health, her own body, particularly in the scene where she is having the bath. She loves sensual things, eating, music, pictures. She has a lot of energy and enthusiasm for things.

What is she like as a person? You should by now, having read the play a few times, have a pretty good idea of Beatie's personality. She is bright, aggressive, full of thought and chatter, but at the same time she has ideals, and feels strongly about things. She's clever and intuitive, but she doesn't rate her own intelligence very highly, and her lack of confidence drags her down.

Choose two or three incidents in the play that seem to you really to show Beatie's personality. Ones you might choose are: when she is tidying Jenny's house; when she gets out of the bath; when she is encouraging her mother to listen to music; when she is challenging the family with the story about the girl. Read through the incidents you have chosen, then make notes on what they show about Beatie. Use these sentences as starting points.

This incident shows that Beatie is . . .
The way she responds to other people tells us that . . .
The ideas she talks about are . . .
The emotions she feels seem to be . . .

For each incident you have picked, choose three or four actual quotations, words from the play which prove a point you are making. Then, using these quotations and the notes you have made, write a paragraph about how each incident shows Beatie's character.

It seems, though, as if sometimes Beatie's character gets lost, because she reflects Ronnie's character so much. She repeats his ideas, quotes his words, copies his gestures. Think about how much of what Beatie says and does is really her, and how much is Ronnie. Does this change later in the play?

Certainly Beatie is very involved with Ronnie. Think back to how she met him, caught him. What does she really feel for him now – is it all admiration, or is there some resentment there? Certainly she seems to be blocking his attempts to help her, as if her individuality is saying, 'stop – I won't be told what to do.' Even so, she seems very dependent on him, and very sure that they have a future together.

Her family are not so sure. They are suspicious of Ronnie. They warn her against him, but she won't listen, and continues believing in him and following him until nearly the end of the play.

How does Beatie react to her family? Over Ronnie, as over most things, she doesn't really listen to them. She sees them as not quite respectable, not up to Ronnie's standards, and she is always concerned that they might let her down. But she does get on better with some of the family than with others. Fill in this chart to show how Beatie feels about these members of her family and how they feel about her – up to the final scene of the play.

Beatie feels about
Her mother
Her father
Jimmy
Jenny

About Beatie

Her mother feels
Her father feels
Jimmy feels
Jenny feels

This, then, is Beatie's relationship with her family for the major part of the play. At the end however, all this changes. When Ronnie breaks off the relationship, Beatie is forced, for the first time, to change. She realizes that, by not developing, by being just as bad as the family she is always complaining about, she has lost Ronnie. At first she blames her family; then, when her mother turns on her, she starts to take responsibility herself. She begins to talk about the need for roots, for culture, the fact that the working class is surrounded by things that are second-rate. And in talking like this, developing her own ideas, she at last does what she has been trying to do all along, have independent thoughts and feelings.

Beatie does break through, but her family doesn't. What do you imagine they are thinking about her as the play finishes, while they are sitting eating their meal? Write four paragraphs, one from the point of view of Mrs Bryant, one each from the points of view of Mr Bryant, Jimmy and Jenny, giving their thoughts as they sit round the table.

By developing as she does, through this crisis, Beatie not only holds our interest; even more importantly, she is a vehicle by which Arnold Wesker explores key ideas. Her relationship holds messages for us about love, sex, marriage. Her interaction with the family shows us certain lessons about family life. Her growth as a person teaches us what an independent woman can be. Her thoughts on the class struggle, and the way she reflects it by her reaction to her family, demonstrate the problems of the working class far more effectively than Ronnie's speeches.

What do you learn from Beatie about all these things? Make a list of some major themes in the play, taking your ideas from this book and adding any other themes you consider important. Then write down what ideas the character of Beatie has given you about these topics.

We have said that Beatie Bryant is the heroine of the play. She is so not only because she is the central point around which all the other characters move; not only because she holds some vital messages about living, which are relevant to all of us; not only because she, of all the characters, changes during the play; she is also the heroine because she is the character we are meant to identify with, and react to, most of all.

How do you react to Beatie; do you admire her, pity her? Do you see any parallels between your life, your experiences and hers; the ways she gets on with her family, how she feels about Ronnie, what she goes through when she is jilted? Do you find anything helpful in what Beatie goes through, and the changes she makes?

Themes

CLASS AND CULTURE

Perhaps one of the most important messages in *Roots* is Arnold Wesker's ideas about the working class. A committed Socialist himself, when he wrote the play he had certain things he wanted to say about the working class, the way they use money, the way they react to culture.

Ask yourself first what is meant by class. Here, it is the working class, those who work for a living with their hands. Certainly everyone sees the Bryants as working class – they themselves, and people like Healey, the manager. Ronnie is probably working class (for Beatie says he slaves all day in a hot kitchen), but he is different from the Bryants because he is part of the 'intelligentsia', those who have learned, by reading and discussion, and who see themselves as the new leaders, who could lead the working class to a position of political power. Beatie herself is working class, but by mixing with Ronnie and his group, she has picked up many ideas that her own working-class family do not have; she still fights Ronnie's ideas though, and in many ways is caught in the middle of the two groups.

Through the Bryants, what is Arnold Wesker telling us about the working class? That the working class is often poor, lives and works in bad conditions, and is powerless to change any of this? These are some of the things he tells us; complete each sentence with proof from the play.

We know that Mr and Mrs Bryant are poor because ...
We know that Jenny and Jimmy are poor because ...
People in the play who live in poor conditions are ...
Many people in the play work at low-paid jobs; examples are ...

Their inability to obtain good working conditions is seen when . . .
Their powerlessness against the bosses is shown when . . .

All of these things are signs of the bad conditions the workers live in, and they may make us want to sympathize with the working class.

Certainly Ronnie, a Socialist, sympathizes with and fights for the working class. Beatie says that he thinks, for example, that the country people live in 'mystic communion with nature', and is sure that Ronnie would get on well with her parents, Stan Mann and all the country people whom she finds so irritating.

Ronnie's ideology holds that the working class should work together to build a new world. He believes that from the working classes should come a new movement, which will rule the country in a fair way, giving decent wages and living conditions, power to the workers, 'human dignity and tolerance and cooperation and equality' (p. 141).

Ronnie also believes in the values of the intelligentsia; in talking deeply, thinking about what is right and wrong, listening to classical music, reading political books and newspapers, looking at paintings. These are things that, as you can see, are not valued in the Bryant household.

When Ronnie goes out with Beatie, then, there are bound to be problems, because of the differences in their background. Which of these sentences summarize their relationship best, in your view?

1. Ronnie likes thinking and talking, and is happy that Beatie is not as good as he is at these things.
2. Beatie is resentful because Ronnie enjoys a culture she cannot understand.
3. Beatie wants to learn about the things Ronnie knows, but is too unintelligent.
4. Ronnie wants to teach Beatie what he knows, but she is too stubborn to learn.
5. Beatie is more intelligent and cultured than Ronnie, and he resents this.

Despite the differences between them, Beatie gradually comes to realize that what Ronnie believes in is important. And when she comes back home to her family, she is faced with a dilemma. Ronnie is the champion of the working class, and that includes her family;

but her own family do not value any of the things that Ronnie admires. They are uncultured, don't understand painting or music, seem unwilling to fight for themselves, and even side with the authorities against strikes.

For example, who says these things – and in what situation? What do they show about the way the Bryants view the world?

'They wanna call us Territorials out – we'd soon break the strike.'

'What's alive about a person that reads books and looks at paintings and listens to classical music?'

'You say Susie's bored, with a radio and television an' that?'

'the world don't want no feelings.'

'it happen all the time.'

Jimmy's argument with Beatie in Act 1, the way the family reacts when Mr Bryant is sacked, and the interchanges between Beatie and her mother about music all serve to convince her, as her home visit continues, that her family may be working class, but they are not admirable.

And so, by the end of the play, when Ronnie finishes the relationship, Beatie is all ready to turn on her family as lacking.

There are several things to remember here, though. As Mrs Bryant points out, Beatie is no better than any of them when it comes to the things she criticizes in her family. She didn't fight for her rights when she was unemployed either – Ronnie did it for her. She read comics rather than books, fought him when he tried to educate her, refused to join in his conversations and arguments. During her relationship with Ronnie, Beatie did not develop, because it was easier not to.

Secondly, in his letter, Ronnie himself admits that a lot of his ideas were wrong. He claims that intellectuals like him could not build a new life for the working classes, or take over the reins of government. He considers that he and his kind are just as powerless as people like the Bryants.

But left to herself, Beatie comes to a new realization, something which Ronnie has not told her, and which gives her a new viewpoint. She realises the importance of 'roots', not in a family sense, but in a cultural sense. She links together ideas that Ronnie has given her with what she has seen with her family and what she has learned herself, to develop the idea that, in order to be fully human, we need to keep in touch with our culture.

And she also realizes that where the working class falls down is that it settles for second-rate culture. It asks for shallow stories, pop music, art that has no real meaning, and so it gets it. In many ways, then, the fact that the working class is stuck in mediocrity is its own fault.

This then is the final lesson of the play, that in order not to be stuck with poverty and powerlessness, the working class has to keep in touch with its roots, and learn really to respond to music, pictures, words and ideas.

Do you agree with this? Do you feel that the music and writing that we are offered today is mostly 'second-rate'? And if so, do you feel that it is holding us back from developing?

FAMILY LIFE

Families can be very different – some just one or two people, some many relatives. They can be immensely close, emotionally involved with each other, or they can meet up rarely and not really know each other as people.

You probably have some clear ideas about what a good family is like. Maybe it is one which leaves you alone, doesn't interfere and lets you be independent. Maybe it is a group of people who support you all the time, and to whom you would always turn when you have a problem.

The family Arnold Wesker shows us in *Roots* is more like the former than the latter. It is the Bryant family for, although Ronnie's family is referred to briefly, it is Beatie's family which is at the centre of the play.

What is the family like? We see almost all of them, except Susan and her husband; Jimmy and Jenny in the first act, Mr and Mrs Bryant in the second, and the family gathered for a welcome party in the third. You should have a good idea of what their relationships are like, how they think members of a family ought to react to one another.

Choose from this list the words and phrases you think best describe the Bryant family relationships. For each, write a few sentences about an incident in the play that illustrates the point. Use quotations, if you can, to prove what you are saying.

unemotional with each other
uncaring
easy and relaxed with each other
always talking
always talking about deep matters
quarrelsome
very supportive when a crisis occurs
willing to go out and fight for each other

Having done this, what impression do you have of the family? Do you think Arnold Wesker wants us to approve of the way they conduct their family life? Which actions does he seem to approve of, and which does he seem to condemn?

Beatie, like Arnold Wesker, seems to find the family 'annoying'. From the time she comes back on a visit, she is constantly picking holes in what they do, comparing the way they live with the way Ronnie lives. She challenges Jenny's ideas of marriage, Jimmy's opinions on strikes. She is always on at her mother to smarten the place up, not to swear, so that she will impress Ronnie when he comes to stay. She is really angry when the family fails to respond to Mr Bryant's sacking. She points out to the family that they are always quarrelling, sometimes not speaking to each other for months or years at a time.

In some ways, however, Beatie enjoys her family. Like all the others, she uses the family situation as a place to relax, eat well, be looked after and comforted. She also enjoys, to a certain extent, the gossip and chatter.

But she does feel that the family, particularly her mother, has let her down by not developing her. In Act 2 and Act 3, we can see her anger at the fact that her family is not as educated or lively as she is, or as Ronnie is. And when she loses Ronnie, her first reaction is to blame her family. She claims that because of them, she was unable to keep him. Her mother retorts that that is her responsibility.

What part do you think a family should play in a person's

development? Do you want your family to be responsible for your growing up – or to leave you strictly alone to develop in the way you want to? Does your family support you in the way you want to be supported – or would you prefer them to act in a different way?

In the end, Beatie seems to agree with her mother, and places the problem further away – on the whole class structure that has made her family as shallow as it is.

But even so, Arnold Wesker is criticizing the Bryant family, not only through Beatie, but also through the words and actions of other people in the play. Mrs Bryant too is resentful, of having to stay and look after her family, when she says she would much rather be independent. Frankie jokes about the 'mighty Bryant clan', and we are aware of how unimpressive the family is. Ronnie's family, despite having a sick father and being emigrés, have lived a far fuller life than the Bryants; his mother, not Beatie's, encourages the girl to develop herself.

At the very end of the play, when Beatie has made her break-through, she calls to the family to share her joy and transformation. But unlike her, they have not broken out of the 'third-rate' trap. When she calls to them, they move away to eat, saying they have had enough.

Beatie is beyond being worried. In the last few minutes of the play, she has grown up, now speaking her own, independent thoughts. And one sign of this independence is that she is no longer affected by what her family thinks.

How does your family compare to the Bryants? Are there any similarities? Any differences? Have you, like Beatie, developed your independence from your family – or do you still feel tied by them and to them? Do you, perhaps, feel that it is not relevant to be independent of your family, who give you so much support and help? For each of us, the situation is different, but whatever your situation is, you may learn something from Beatie and her family.

LOVE, SEX AND MARRIAGE

The climax of *Roots* is the breaking up of an engagement: even so, it is certainly a play that revolves around the idea of intimate relationships. Arnold Wesker presents us with a whole series of viewpoints about what love means, the place of sexuality, and what a marriage is.

First of all, then, look at how many relationships we meet in the play. Beatie's relationship with Ronnie, and its subsequent break-up, dominates, including love, sex and proposed marriage. Jimmy and Jenny, Mr and Mrs Bryant, and Frankie and Pearl are also married, with varying types of relationship, though at least one of those couples would probably not consider 'love' part of their marriage. Stan Mann and his lady, on the other hand, did not marry, though their relationship was close. Neither did Jenny and the man with whom she had sex, and a child. Can you think of any other relationships mentioned, however briefly?

Certainly the issue of sexuality seems to be the most straightforward in the play. The country people indulge in sex, enjoy it, joke about it even when old. Sometimes they are remarkably embarrassed by talking about it – Jenny and Jimmy are taken aback when Beatie mentions 'love in the afternoon'. In general, though, it seems an easy thing, without strong emotion, as natural as animals breeding. Even Beatie comments that Ronnie (not she) thought that sex brought responsibility for the person slept with.

In Act 3, there are two specific comments about sex – one when Frankie mentions the society for the sexually frustrated, the other when Beatie tells the story of the girl living by the river. The members of the family react in a variety of ways, and you should already be aware of the differing opinions – shock, tolerance, lack of understanding. Compare these with your own opinions; how would you have reacted if these conversations had taken place when you were in the room? And how would your judgement have compared with those of the characters in the play?

The three main viewpoints on marriage that we see are those of Mr and Mrs Bryant, an established marriage, Jenny and Jimmy, a new marriage, and Beatie and Ronnie, who are thinking of marriage.

Beatie seems to have a rather unrealistic view of the married state: '. . . once we're married and I got babies, I won't need to be interested in half the things I got to be interested in now . . .' (p. 96). We're not sure how Ronnie sees marriage, but certainly by the end of the play he does not see Beatie as a future wife.

Jimmy and Jenny have a realistic, down-to-earth relationship, based on running a house, bringing up children and giving each other mutual support.

For Mr and Mrs Bryant, after many years of marriage, the relationship is settled, unemotional, and stable despite problems of money and quarrels.

Draw up a grid with the names of each couple at the top. Along the side write these questions. Then fill the grid in.

1. What does each person in the couple get from being married or considering being married?
2. What problems does marriage, or the thought of it, create?
3. What hopes does each person have of their married life in the future?

Read through what you have written, and then consider which relationship, if any, you consider is a good one. Would you want to be part of any of these marriages?

You yourself may be engaged, married, or know people who are. What is your, or their, ideal of marriage? Is it very different from the almost business-like partnership that the Norfolk couples seem to imagine?

One element that certainly doesn't seem to be a part of the married couples' relationship is love. Mr and Mrs Bryant don't speak of it. Jenny comments that she doesn't believe in it, and presumably then Jimmy doesn't either.

Beatie, though, talks a lot about love. Read through her major speeches and then write a paragraph, as if you were Beatie, on what you mean by love. Does Beatie's view differ from your own personal view? Do you like her idea of love?

Certainly her family and friends worry about Beatie's ideas of love and relationships. They think that her engagement is doomed to disaster. Which characters hold the views

1. that Ronnie and Beatie have little in common, so will not be happy?
2. that Ronnie doesn't appreciate what Beatie does for him?
3. that the fact Ronnie is so different in background from Beatie means the relationship will have problems?

You can see that the family's idea of a successful relationship is not Beatie's. They look for partners of similar background, who will do things for them, and work together to form a partnership. There are quarrels and disagreements, money problems and power struggles, but the marriage goes on. Emotions are not an issue, and Beatie's highly emotional references to love don't mean anything to them.

Beatie clings on to her ideas, but when Ronnie jilts her, we see that her emotions were not enough to keep them together. In fact, when we read Ronnie's letter, we discover that he too was looking for a sort of partnership. He doesn't refer to emotion, or love; in fact he uses the word 'romantic' in a critical sense. Instead, he talks about building a world together, teaching and learning. Beatie realizes that it is her inability to be a partner to him, to work with him, not against him, that has doomed the relationship. She cannot yet support her loved one, as Stan Mann's lady has done, as Ronnie's mother has done – and so her love is only an emotion, not a real force.

Do you think Beatie loved Ronnie? Does she respect him? Look at the evidence from her own words and actions, and also from Ronnie's letter? Does he love her – what does she think, what does her family think? What does Ronnie himself think, do you imagine?

In a later play by Arnold Wesker, we meet Ronnie himself, and he makes a passing comment on his relationship with Beatie. 'You can't change people . . . you can only give them love and hope they'll take it . . . Beatie Bryant took it but nothing seemed to happen' (*Talking About Jerusalem*, Act 2). Do you agree with Ronnie's comment on the relationship? Do you think Beatie would agree with it?

Whose fault is it that the relationship fails? Perhaps it is Ronnie's. Perhaps it is Beatie's. Perhaps it is no one's fault at all. Write three paragraphs, each taking one of these three viewpoints. When you have finished, ask yourself which opinion you now hold.

At the end of the play then, it seems as if the judgement has come down on the side of an unemotional partnership as being the best kind of relationship. The Bryants, like Stan Mann and his lady, will stay together until death, despite their quarrels. Jimmy and Jenny will do the same, bringing up their children and supporting each other. Beatie, who put all her emotion into 'love', will end up, like the girl in the moral tale, without anyone.

However, maybe it is not as clear as this. For however sensible the marriages in the play are, and however logical Ronnie's breaking-off is, it is Beatie who keeps our interest and our sympathy. We cannot doubt that a relationship with Beatie, complete with her problems, would be more interesting than with Jenny or Mrs Bryant. So perhaps Beatie's ideals of love are not so silly after all. What do you think?

THE PLACE OF WOMEN

Women are very important in *Roots*. The main character is a woman, and she is surrounded by other women who challenge, side with or oppose her. Despite being a man, Arnold Wesker has written a play which supports women and their self-development.

The world in which the play is set is one in which women seem to live a very traditional life. Read these descriptions of the ways women behave and are treated in that world, and see which ones seem most true to you and which do not.

1. Women look after the home.
2. Women make decisions about the important things in life.
3. Women do not usually take jobs outside the home.
4. Women gossip and talk about each other.
5. Women quarrel with each other.
6. Women are dependent on men for survival.
7. Women do not have control over the money.
8. Women are equal in sexual matters.
9. Women are partners to their men.
10. Women are wrapped up in their own domestic lives.

Once you have a general picture of life as a woman in that situation, write a paragraph about it. Would you have liked to have been a woman in the place and time *Roots* is set? Can you see any advantages, any disadvantages?

The women in the play all live the sort of life we have described. We hear about some of them – Susan, Stan Mann's 'wife' – and meet four more – Pearl, Jenny, Mrs Bryant, Beatie. Apart from Beatie, all the women live in Norfolk with their husbands, all have little chance of ever changing their situation.

What sort of people are these women? Do they seem independent? In physical terms, no. Mrs Bryant has no say over how the money is spent, Jenny seems quite content to keep house for Jimmy and her child. What other examples can you find in the play of women being financially or physically dependent on others?

But in some ways, these women are very strong and self-sufficient. 'Mrs Mann' devotes herself to Stan, bravely giving up her job to do so. Jimmy and Jenny seem partners in the business of being a family. Mrs Bryant is a capable woman, able to face her husband's unemployment without panicking.

All, in their different ways, seem to be (or have been) at ease with sex in a way many of their 'liberated' sisters might envy. We see Mrs Bryant joking with Stan Mann, and happily continuing a friendship with a man convicted of accosting men. Jenny, having had an illegitimate child herself, easily responds to Jimmy's suggestion of a club for the sexually frustrated with an insinuation that women need more sex than men do.

Beatie is the woman who, unlike the others, has left home, mixed with the intelligentsia, lived with a man, and might be expected to be more independent, more liberated. She has had the example of Ronnie's mother, one of the few women mentioned in the play who seems to be living the sort of life Beatie wants (and even she is tied down by a sick husband).

Is Beatie like this though? She still seems dependent on people. She looks to her mother, blaming her when things go wrong. She has no more control over her father than Mrs Bryant has. She cannot fight for herself when she is unemployed.

Look too at the way she talks about Ronnie, the way she quotes him and talks about him. She is, in fact, far more emotionally dependent on her partner than country relatives are on theirs. Find at least five examples of things Beatie says or does that show she is emotionally dependent on Ronnie.

In addition, she is not really living the sort of life she wants. She can neither break free of Ronnie nor turn the relationship into what she wants it to be. Jenny at least has gone for what she wants, an uncomplicated partnership with someone with whom she can have children and make a home. Beatie on the other hand has not got the relationship she wants – and, at the end of the play, does not even have the relationship she doesn't want.

What do you think the other women characters think about Beatie?

Complete these sentences, as if they were spoken by characters in the play, to show what you think other women think of Beatie.

Mrs Bryant: She may think she's grown up, but . . .
Jenny: She seems like a self-sufficient woman, but . . .
Pearl: She says she is going to get married, but . . .

What do you think Beatie thinks of the lives the other women in her family live? Write a paragraph as if you were Beatie, saying what you think about Pearl, Jenny and Mrs Bryant.

And how do the men view the women? Think about the major male characters in the play – Ronnie, Jimmy, Mr Bryant. How do they view the Bryant women? Jimmy and Mr Bryant expect their wives to look after them, but does this mean they don't respect and love them too?

And Ronnie – does he consider Beatie to be independent or just stubborn? He certainly seems to try to change her and her character – but do you think he is trying to change her, to dominate her, or is he trying to do the best for her?

When Ronnie jilts Beatie, two major things happen. Mrs Bryant suddenly loses patience, and turns on Beatie – and we learn from this that she is not so happy with her role and would like, if she could, to leave the home and work. But do you think she really means this, or is it only said in anger? Think about this, and then write a paragraph on your view.

We also see changes in Beatie. Up to now, she has been dependent for her self-esteem, even her very ideas and words, on the support of her family and Ronnie. Jilted, she turns to her family, gets nothing, and then blames them. But she soon starts taking responsibility for what has happened, and makes the transition from a dependent child who blames everyone but herself to a self-sufficient woman who can face up to what has happened and realize where she has gone wrong.

And in fact being jilted makes Beatie reach a new stage in her development, for she very soon starts to have unique, independent ideas. Her last words in the play, when the family ignores her, and she is aware that Ronnie is no longer there to support her, are her own words, the start of her new life as an independent woman – 'I'm beginning, on my own two feet – I'm beginning . . .' (p. 148).

PASSAGES FOR COMPARISON

MARRIAGE

... When she introduces me to her parents
back straightened, hair finally combed, strangled by a tie,
Should I sit knees together on their 3rd degree sofa
and not ask Where's the bathroom?
How else to feel other than I am,
often thinking Flash Gordon soap —
O how terrible it must be for a young man
seated before a family and the family thinking
We never saw him before! He wants our Mary Lou!
After tea and homemade cookies they ask
What do you do for a living?
Should I tell them? Would they like me then?
Say All right get married, we're not losing a daughter
we're gaining a son —
And should I then ask Where's the bathroom?

Gregory Corso, *Penguin Modern Poets 5*

SOMETIME IT HAPPENS

And sometimes it happens that you are friends and
   then
You are not friends.
And friendship has passed.
And whole days are lost and among them
A fountain empties itself.

And sometimes it happens that you are loved and
   then
You are not loved,
And love is past.

And whole days are lost and among them
A fountain empties itself into the grass.

And sometimes you want to speak to her and then
You do not want to speak.
Then the opportunity has passed.
Your dreams flare up, they suddenly vanish.

And also it happens that there is nowhere to go and
* then*
There is somewhere to go,
Then you have bypassed.
And the years flare up and are gone.
Quicker than a minute.

So you have nothing.
You wonder if these things matter and then
They cease to matter,
And caring is past.
And a fountain empties itself into the grass.

Brian Patten, *Vanishing Trick*

WINTER

We've been together now for forty years,
An' it don't seem a day too much;
There ain't a lady livin' in the land
As 'd swop for my dear old Dutch.

I calls 'er Sal;
'Er proper name is Sairer;
An' yer may find a gal
As you'd consider fairer.
She ain't a angel – she can start
A-jawin' till it makes yer smart;
She's just a woman, bless 'er 'eart,
* Is my old gal . . .*

We've been together now for forty years.

An' it don't seem a day too much;
There ain't a lady livin' in the land
As 'd swop for my dear old Dutch.

   I sees yer, Sal –
Yer pretty ribbons sportin';
Many years now, old gal,
Since them young days of courtin'.
I ain't a coward, still I trust
When we've to part, as part we must,
That Death may come and take me fust
   To wait ... my pal.

Albert Chevalier, *My Old Dutch*, 1892

THE EARLY MARRIED LIFE OF THE MORELS

'Good gracious,' she cried, 'coming home in his drunkenness!'

'Comin' home in his what?' he snarled, his hat over his eye. Suddenly her blood rose in a jet.

'Say you're *not* drunk!' she flashed.

She had put down her saucepan, and was stirring the sugar into the beer. He dropped his two hands heavily on the table, and thrust his face forwards at her.

'"Say you're not drunk,"' he repeated. 'Why, nobody but a nasty little bitch like you 'ud 'ave such a thought.'

He thrust his face forward at her.

'There's money to bezzle with, if there's money for nothing else.'

'I've not spent a two-shillin' bit this day,' he said.

'You don't get as drunk as a lord on nothing,' she replied. 'And,' she cried, flashing into sudden fury, 'if you've been sponging on your beloved Jerry, why, let him look after his children for they need it.'

'It's a lie, it's a lie. Shut your face, woman.'

They were now at battle-pitch. Each forgot everything save the hatred of the other and the battle between them. She was fiery and furious as he. They went on till he called her a liar.

'No,' she cried, starting up, scarce able to breathe. 'Don't call me that – you, the most despicable liar that ever walked in shoe-leather.' She forced the last words out of suffocated lungs.

'You're a liar!' he yelled, banging the table with his fist. 'You're a liar, you're a liar.'

She stiffened herself, with clenched fists.

'The house is filthy with you,' she cried.

'Then get out on it – it's mine. Get out on it!' he shouted. 'It's me as brings th' money whoam, not thee. It's my house, not thine. Then ger out on't – ger out on't!'

'And I would,' she cried, suddenly shaken into tears of impotence. 'Ah, wouldn't I, wouldn't I have gone long ago, but for those children. Ay, haven't I repented not going years ago, when I'd only the one' – suddenly drying into rage. 'Do you think it's for *you* I stop – do you think I'd stop one minute for *you*?'

'Go, then,' he shouted, beside himself. 'Go!'

'No!' She faced round. 'No,' she cried loudly, 'you shan't have it *all* your own way; you shan't do *all* you like. I've got those children to see to. My word,' she laughed, 'I should look well to leave them to you.'

'Go,' he cried thickly, lifting his fist. He was afraid of her. 'Go!'

D. H. Lawrence, *Sons and Lovers*

Glossary

As you may notice from the pronunciation note at the beginning of the play, the characters speak in Norfolk accent and intonation. So even when they are using words that are part of most people's everyday speech, we may not recognize these words, either when we hear them in the performed play or read them in the written text. This glossary includes many of these words, with their Standard English equivalents. It also includes other words and their definitions. It is also useful to bear in mind the points made in the pronunciation note.

'em: them
'fore: before
'n: than
'nough: enough
'sides: besides
'spect: I expect
'tent: isn't
'twere: it were
a'tween: between
a-lookin': looking
abide: bear
accosting: attacking
afeared: afraid
aggressive: attacking
allotment: plot of land for farming
'an: than
articulate: able to speak
association: society
audible: able to be heard

barmy: mad
bin: been
blust: blast

bor: neighbour, person, boy, an affectionate term

clan: family
clobber: gear
contemplate: look at thoughtfully
copper: copper water heater
cos: because
cossack dance: fast Russian dance
could've: could have

daf: daft, silly
dickey suit: nakedness
ditched: left in the lurch
don': don't
dowsin': drenching
driv: drive

emerge: come out
ensue: follow
ent: haven't
ent: isn't

euphemistically: using a mild expression in place of a realistic one

fiendish: devilish
fist: first
frilling: decoration
fret: worry
furse: first

gaiters: covering for ankle or lower leg
gimme: give me
git: get
give 'em no heed: take no notice of
glass cherries: glacé cherries
glee: childish happiness
gonna: going to
gore: pierce with a horn
gotta: got to
gouache: opaque colours ground with water and thickened with gum
grub: food
grumpy: ill-tempered

hed: had
hev: have
hevn't: haven't
hinder: get in the way, stop
his-self: himself
hooligan: vandal
intonation: tone of speaking
jive: dance

Labour Tote: equivalent of the Pools
ligament: fibre binding bones together
lip: cheek, answering back

manny: man
mighty: large, important

mount: have sex with
mowld: mould
mystic: spiritual

narthin': nothing
no: any

o': of
observation: comment
ole: old
on: can be used as 'of'
ont: won't
owle: old

paralytic: as if paralysed
patch: patch of ground
pick-up: portable record-player
primitive: simple, with primary colours
proclamation: announcement

ramshackle: tumbledown
reserve: control
retrieve: fetch
riled: upset, angry
ruddy: red
rum: strange
runners: runner beans

shant: shan't
shrivelled: wrinkled
shut you up: shut up, be quiet
signifying: showing
skiffle: modern music
skint: make do on little money
snob: person with too much respect for his superiors
snub: put down
soon ever: as soon as
squit: rubbish, nonsense
stagnate: become dull and sluggish

stoop: bow or bend
struck on: keen on

take heed: take notice, listen
Territorials: reserve army
thaas: that is
the club: mail order
tied cottage: cottage that goes with a job

un: one
unabashed: unashamed
utility: functional, useful

vigorously: actively

wan': want
wanna: want to, ought to
watcha: how are you, what have you
whatta: what to
wi': with
windsor-type: wooden furniture with curved support for arms and back

yearp: yes
yit: yet

FOR THE BEST IN PAPERBACKS, LOOK FOR THE

In every corner of the world, on every subject under the sun, Penguins represent quality and variety – the very best in publishing today.

For complete information about books available from Penguin and how to order them, write to us at the appropriate address below. Please note that for copyright reasons the selection of books varies from country to country.

In the United Kingdom: For a complete list of books available from Penguin in the U.K., please write to *Dept EP, Penguin Books Ltd, Harmondsworth, Middlesex, UB7 0DA*

In the United States: For a complete list of books available from Penguin in the U.S., please write to *Dept BA, Viking Penguin, 299 Murray Hill Parkway, East Rutherford, New Jersey 07073*

In Canada: For a complete list of books available from Penguin in Canada, please write to *Penguin Books Canada Limited, 2801 John Street, Markham, Ontario L3R 1B4*

In Australia: For a complete list of books available from Penguin in Australia, please write to the *Marketing Department, Penguin Books Australia Ltd, P.O. Box 257, Ringwood, Victoria 3134*

In New Zealand: For a complete list of books available from Penguin in New Zealand, please write to the *Marketing Department, Penguin Books (N.Z.) Ltd, Private Bag, Takapuna, Auckland 9*

In India: For a complete list of books available from Penguin in India, please write to *Penguin Overseas Ltd, 706 Eros Apartments, 56 Nehru Place, New Delhi 110019*

FOR THE BEST IN PAPERBACKS, LOOK FOR THE

PLAYS IN PENGUIN

Edward Albee **Who's Afraid of Virginia Woolf?**

Alan Ayckbourn **The Norman Conquests**

Bertolt Brecht **Parables for the Theatre (The Good Woman of Setzuan/The Caucasian Chalk Circle)**

Anton Chekhov **Plays (The Cherry Orchard/The Three Sisters/Ivanov/The Seagull/Uncle Vanya)**

Michael Hastings **Tom and Viv**

Henrik Ibsen **Hedda Gabler/Pillars of Society/The Wild Duck**

Eugène Ionesco **Absurd Drama (Rhinoceros/The Chair/The Lesson)**

Ben Jonson **Three Comedies (Volpone/The Alchemist/Bartholomew Fair)**

D. H. Lawrence **Three Plays (The Collier's Friday Night/The Daughter-in-Law/The Widowing of Mrs Holroyd)**

Arthur Miller **Death of a Salesman**

John Mortimer **A Voyage Round My Father/What Shall We Tell Caroline?/The Dock Brief**

J. B. Priestley **Time and the Conways/I Have Been Here Before/An Inspector Calls/The Linden Tree**

Peter Shaffer **Amadeus**

Bernard Shaw **Plays Pleasant (Arms and the Man/Candida/The Man of Destiny/You Never Can Tell)**

Sophocles **Three Theban Plays (Oedipus the King/Antigone/Oedipus at Colonus)**

Arnold Wesker **The Wesker Trilogy (Chicken Soup with Barley/Roots/I'm Talking about Jerusalem)**

Oscar Wilde **Plays (Lady Windermere's Fan/A Woman of No Importance/An Ideal Husband/The Importance of Being Earnest/Salome)**

Thornton Wilder **Our Town/The Skin of Our Teeth/The Matchmaker**

Tennessee Williams **Sweet Bird of Youth/A Streetcar Named Desire/The Glass Menagerie**

FOR THE BEST IN PAPERBACKS, LOOK FOR THE

PENGUIN PASSNOTES

This comprehensive series, designed to help O-level and CSE students, includes:

SUBJECTS
Biology
Chemistry
Economics
English Language
French
Geography
Human Biology
Mathematics
Modern Mathematics
Modern World History
Narrative Poems
Physics

SHAKESPEARE
As You Like It
Henry IV, Part I
Henry V
Julius Caesar
Macbeth
The Merchant of Venice
A Midsummer Night's Dream
Romeo and Juliet
Twelfth Night

LITERATURE
Arms and the Man
Cider With Rosie
Great Expectations
Jane Eyre
Kes
Lord of the Flies
A Man for All Seasons
The Mayor of Casterbridge
My Family and Other Animals
Pride and Prejudice
The Prologue to The Canterbury
    Tales
Pygmalion
Saint Joan
She Stoops to Conquer
Silas Marner
To Kill a Mockingbird
War of the Worlds
The Woman in White
Wuthering Heights